The Mother Cabrini
Companion

Mother Cabrini

The Mother Cabrini Companion

A Spiritual Journey with a Courageous Woman of God
Edited by Kristen Van Uden Theriault

SOPHIA INSTITUTE PRESS
Manchester, New Hampshire

Mother Cabrini's words quoted in this book were previously published in *Travels of Mother Frances Xavier Cabrini*, 1944 by the Missionary Sisters of the Sacred Heart of Jesus Chicago, Illinois and in *Journal of a Trusting Heart: Retreat Notes of St. Frances Cabrini*, 1984 by the Missionary Sisters of the Sacred Heart, Sacred Heart Novitiate, Philadelphia, PA.

Printed in the United States of America. All rights reserved.

Cover design by Emma Helstrom

Cover image: Copyright © 2024 by Angel Studios

Sophia Institute Press
Box 5284, Manchester, NH 03108
1-800-888-9344
www.SophiaInstitute.com

Sophia Institute Press is a registered trademark of Sophia Institute.

paperback ISBN 979-8-88911-328-7

ebook ISBN 979-8-88911-329-4

Library of Congress Control Number: 2024933323

First printing

Contents

Contents

Foreword

Who was St. Frances Xavier Cabrini?

This is a question worth asking because she is a woman worth knowing.

Some of us may recognize her name attached to orphanages, hospitals, and institutions of public services in large American cities such as New York and Chicago. Though she lived and died more than a century ago, what might Mother Cabrini—as she was known in her day—have to say to us today?

This valiant woman has so much to teach us—from her deep devotion to Christ and His Sacred Heart, to the strength she derived from the Eucharist to overcome the obstacles that stood in her way, to her humble obedience to the Lord and His Church to be His hands and feet in the world. She had an indefatigable resolve to make God's loving mercy present in a tangible way to the poor, the sick, the orphaned, and the immigrants, and it changed America and changed the world.

She is a woman worth listening to, and there is no better way to come to know St. Frances Xavier Cabrini than by reflecting upon her own words and allowing this courageous woman of God to take us on a spiritual journey. From her earliest desire to be a missionary and to save souls for Christ, to her journeys across the ocean, to her work in the many houses she founded in the United States and throughout the world, Mother Cabrini prepared a treasure trove of personal journals and letters written to her daughters. These were the many women who, attracted by her way of life and service, joined the Missionary Sisters of the Sacred Heart, the religious order she founded, which still carries on Mother Cabrini's mission on six continents across the globe.

Her words of prayer, reflection, devotion, inspiration, and encouragement resonate today as if they were written to us. May this collection of her writings capture your heart, inspire in you a renewed desire for the Lord, and strengthen you to respond to Christ with the same confidence of Mother Cabrini: "If Thou wish it, it can be done."

– *Emily Wilson Hussem, International speaker and author*

The Mother Cabrini
Companion

Introduction

Heaven in Her Heart

By Kristen Van Uden Theriault

*If the Sacred Heart would give me the means I would
construct a boat called "The House of Cristoforo"
("Bearer of Christ") to traverse with one Community,
little or big, so as to carry the Name of Christ to
all people, to those who as yet do not know Him,
and also to those who have forgotten Him.*

So writes Mother Cabrini, the tenacious saint whose great zeal for souls led her across oceans and continents to spread the Word of God.

The scale at which Mother alleviated human suffering is unmatched. Throughout her lifetime, her Missionary Sisters of the Sacred Heart of Jesus established sixty-seven institutions dedicated to serving schoolchildren, orphans, and the poor. The scope of these missions made her order one of the farthest reaching and impactful of its day.

Mother Cabrini's vocation transcended humanitarian concerns, being first and foremost concerned with the salvation of the *souls* of all she served. She was driven by a supernatural charity that was always fixed on Heaven.

Her personal writings reveal this zeal for souls in an intimate way. As she writes, she had "Heaven in her heart," and she sought to project this beatific bliss to the most lost and isolated of God's sheep. Indifferent to background or socioeconomic status, she treated each person she encountered as a dignified child of God, always with an eye to deeper conversion.

Her great devotion to the Sacred Heart was the impetus for her love of souls: she loved them as Jesus loves. As she comments in a letter of encouragement to her sisters, "Your love must be active as that of Jesus on Golgotha. 'Sitio,' 'I thirst,' cried Jesus, 'for souls.'"

She recognized that the missionary's primary work was to continue Jesus' divine mission:

> There was a time when Our Lord went through the streets of Jerusalem drawing souls to Himself by His Divine looks; but, to-day, it is by His spirit and His loving Heart that He draws souls to His following and inflames them. My Jesus, how good Thou art! I shall never cease to speak of Thee and Thy Divine Heart! I shall never tire of proclaiming Thy praises, so that Thou risest every day like a bright and ardent lamp and run as a Giant in every country, enlightening souls, warming up hearts, drawing them into the fold of Thy Church and helping them to follow Thee more closely.

Dedicated to illustrious patrons such as St. Francis Xavier, whose name she took by the addition of "Saverio" to her given name, Francesca, Mother envisioned missionary work as truly apostolic, separated only by time:

> "You are the light of the world, the salt of the earth," Jesus said, when from the mountain He spoke to His Apostles. And you, Missionaries of the Sacred Heart, belong in a certain measure to the Apostolic family.

Have you not to continue the Apostolate of the great
Mission of Christ? To you also is entrusted the Mission
of being the salt of the earth and the light of the world.

Like Our Lady, Mother Cabrini was always concerned with reflecting Jesus in all her actions, with *being* Jesus to others: from her
neighbor to the souls of the Far East that she so wished to save.

The urgency and energy of Mother's actions make evident that
she understood the immediacy of the missionary vocation in our
short sojourn in this vale of tears. She instructs her sisters:

The days fly, souls are being lost. Death is approaching
more quickly than we realize, and then the time for
work is over. Work, then, while you have time. Work
with energy, and especially with the spirit of sacrifice,
for it is this that forms the true Missionary. This storms
the Heart of Jesus, and draws from It, as it were, the
most precious graces for those souls who are the hardest and the most obstinate in resisting His love. Work
with an apostolic spirit which offers everything, actions,
prayers and sacrifices for the conversion of souls.

Indeed, the magnitude of her ambitious work would have been
impossible if not for supernatural means. Her simple yet profound
trust in God enabled her to overcome worldly roadblocks. Mother
Cabrini's childlike faith in God's Providence lent her confidence
to conquer the world in love, embodying her contemporary Pope
St. Pius X's injunction to "restore all things in Christ."

Mother writes, assertively:

The Missionary knows no distance—the world is so
small. Space is an imperceptible object to a Missionary, because she is accustomed to dwell on eternity,

to which she wishes to conduct all the souls she can—those souls which have been redeemed by the Most Precious Blood of Jesus Christ.

The missionary's role is not just to preach the Gospel and gain Baptisms, but to facilitate the religious development of the whole person, setting the foundation for lifelong devotion. Catholic education was a cornerstone of Mother Cabrini's mission: solid formation is essential to equip the soul for a life well lived.

In true missionary spirit, Mother recognized that conversion is not merely a one-time choice, but an ongoing process, requiring constant conversion of heart and rededication to the Divine Will. Even in her advanced spiritual development, she saw room for continual growth:

> To-day the skin has begun to peel off my forehead and nose. I am changing like a serpent. God wants me to change my life and be converted; to confirm this, my dearest daughters, pray. The Sacred Heart of Jesus will always hear favourably the prayers of children for their Mother. Pray! Pray! I am in need of your intercession. When I am converted and begin to lead a good life, it is certain that this will obtain many beautiful graces for the Institute.

She thus echoes St. Paul, who also advised continual inner conversion:

> So we do not lose heart. Though our outer nature is wasting away, our inner nature is being renewed every day. For this slight momentary affliction is preparing for us an eternal weight of glory beyond all comparison, because we look not to the things that are seen

but to the things that are unseen; for the things that are seen are transient, but the things that are unseen are eternal. (2 Cor. 4:16-18)

Mother Cabrini considered the entire world her frontier, but she never neglected the infinite frontier within her own heart, drawing ever closer to her Savior.

Perhaps the most beautiful of Mother's writings are her meditations on Heaven and eternity, always keeping in mind the ultimate end of all missionary work.

The beauty of creation, particularly the sea, which Mother had ample opportunity to study on her dozens of transatlantic voyages, prompts poetic musings:

> We seem to see the portals of Heaven which do not close at the end of the day, because there daytime never ends, for the day up there is eternal and the light which emanates from the Divine Face never fails. There, in that abode, exists no night, no ignorance, no blindness, for everything is seen in God; there, no sorrows exist, no tears, no adversity, no sighs. No, daughters, in Heaven there are no clouds to obscure the Divine Sun, the Eternal Sun of Justice. There is no fear of losing God; no wiles of the enemy, for he has been routed; the world is far away, and the body spiritualized lives in harmony with the soul. No, there is no night in Heaven and the door is always open. Friends reach there at every moment, every instant; they do not disturb, but, rather, render the repose serene and sweet.

Mother always accompanies these musings with intercessory prayer and practical advice for saving souls, truly uniting the missionary's temporal work in the Church Militant to her eventual home in the Church Triumphant:

> Oh, sublime City, send down your beams of Light to these regions of darkness, this shadow of death where we still miserably live. Come, oh Supernatural Light, to reveal to us the beauties of that Blessed Country, and detach us from the miseries of this earth; make our eyes so pure that, through the shining crystal of Faith, they may behold the eternal good which awaits us after a short time of sacrifice and self-conquering. He who fights will be victorious, and to the victor the prize is Heaven.

What emerges from Mother Cabrini's words is a portrait of a soul completely at *peace* but never at *rest*: she did indeed have Heaven in her heart and worked tirelessly to share the joys of God's eternal love, expanding the Kingdom of Heaven in the frontier of souls.

I hope you enjoy this curated selection of some of the most insightful writings of this joyful saint.

—KVT

Week 1

Detachment

Let all your affections, my daughters, be centred in this beautiful Heart, and you will always be happy; but if, instead, you foster private affections that tie you to self, or to creatures, you will always have annoyances, hours of disgust and melancholy. Free yourselves, and put on wings, I pray you, in order that you may rise above the earth.

$$\backsim$$

Oh, my daughters, what an excellent thing is a pure soul detached from everything and from self! She can bury herself in God, Who is the source of all courage. Let us then become pure, simple, unpretentious, raised above all created things. When we have achieved this, we shall begin to realise that true happiness which has awaited us this long time and is in store for us if we wish it.

$$\backsim$$

Let us work, day by day, in the Lord's vineyard, seeking the greater glory of God, in perfect detachment from everything, which is of very great importance to ourselves, for often without our knowing it, we are the enemies of our own souls, troubling ourselves about many things, whilst "Porro unum est necessarium."

$$\backsim$$

We also made a little meditation on the beautiful lesson of Saint Bernard, wherein he speaks of the force and power of the love of God in a soul, and how the possession of this love enables a soul not to feel further the weight of any cross, which rather becomes a great pleasure and delight.

∞

Oh, happy the soul that lives in the true love of Christ! My daughters, detach yourselves from all persons and all things, and you will have a foretaste of the Paradise of true, solid and Heavenly love.

My Thoughts and Prayers

Week 2

Meditations on the
Beauty of Creation

This morning we went to visit and pay our respects to the Captain and Commissioner. They listened with great courtesy, and offered their help in all our needs. These persons did not know us, but they were so kind to us. From this we can learn to appreciate the great love the Heart of Jesus has for His Spouses. He heaps upon us benefits and favours we do not merit. Let us be ever grateful, so that gratitude may obtain for us greater graces. This morning we went on deck, saluted the sea, the image of the immensity of God, then we recited our prayers, which, without effort, came fervently from our souls. We then recited the Ave Maris Stella. We did not sing because we were afraid of disturbing the other passengers on board, but the Most Holy Virgin, who had blessed our departure, listened to the melody of the affections of her devout daughters, if not the melody of their voices.

How many beautiful thoughts the calmness of the sea suggests. We see in it the happiness of a soul that lives in the tranquillity of the grace of God. In such a fortunate soul all is calm; peace undisturbed; it has the capacity of raising itself to the sublimity of the Divine mysteries. This gives us a vision of the immensity of the power of God, Who commands this endless sea, which could rise in whirling billows, while on the contrary it remains calm and tranquil.

God commands, the sea obeys. If also in Religion every Sister would obey her Superior, with perfect submission that is, without relying on her own judgment, what calmness, what tranquillity, what a sweetness of Paradise would be hers! My daughters! Act in this way, be obedient, be most humble, not having your own judgment, submitting with great peace and simplicity to your Superiors, and there will be in your Houses a true anticipated Paradise which will precede the eternal one which awaits you.

It seems as if Jesus Himself has said to the sea, "Peace be with you." Hence this is a figure of a pure soul, without wrath, who leaves all, and is united exclusively with her beloved and Divine Spouse; reposing on His left arm while with the right He caresses her.

My Thoughts and Prayers

Week 3

God the Creator

At the sight of the sea many beautiful thoughts and feelings arise within one. The sky is blue and the horizon is vast. It is the image of the love of God when it takes possession of a soul and makes it capable of an immensity of holy deeds.

Yes! Grace is an infinite treasure of God and those who receive it, and make good use of it, are truly partakers of the friendship of God. Is it not precious for the immense increase which at every hour it makes in our souls? It is true, then, that the ocean is a beautiful image of grace.

Let us try, oh, my daughters, to attract the grace of God to our souls, by perfect detachment of all and from all, even from our most ardent desires that may disturb the peace and quietness of soul, which are the fruits of grace.

I write after having assisted at a spectacle quite new to myself and also new to some of the sailors. About eleven o'clock we saw ourselves surrounded by enormous masses of ice. At first they appeared to be things of no importance, like white doves resting on the water, but afterwards, little by little, they grew much larger.

They took enormous proportions, and when we got
nearer to them we saw that they were about twelve times
larger than our ship. The Captain reduced the speed of
the engines and took a different route to avoid them,
but for all that at one moment we were only a distance
of about sixty yards from them. Now we see some of
them in the distance. We feel afraid of the coming
night. Perhaps, then, there will be danger, but we leave
ourselves in the Hands of the good Jesus.

The marvellous spectacle, which is continually present
to our vision, offers us a good preparation for Holy
Communion, as we all see this is the work of Him,
Whom we so ardently desire to welcome in the small
Sanctuary of our souls.

It is true the weather is cold just like an April morning, but the air is pure and it is a pleasure to breathe
it. It is healthy and inspires sublime thoughts, just as
a celestial ray would surround us and raise our minds
to that God, so good, so dear, and so great. He has
made so many beautiful things for us, poor creatures,
the work of His omnipotent Hand.

My Thoughts and Prayers

Week 4

Creation Mirrors the Soul

This morning I saw marvellous fishes of many colors joyfully basking in the sea, just as our souls should bask in the grace of God.

∞

Yesterday the sea looked like a soul, agitated by remorse and pride, who never finds peace with God.

∞

To-day is the 15th; we have been more fortunate, we do not feel as if we were at sea, but rather wrapped up in a cloud like that of the Transfiguration. There is a charming blue sky above, and below us one can hardly distinguish the sea from the sky. Some of the passengers say we are in the third heavens, others, the seventh; the glorious splendour renders everything so bright and brilliant that the passengers exclaim, "How lovely, how beautiful."

∞

The sea continues calm and wonderfully tranquil. It seems to reflect the peace and the features of a soul adorned with sanctifying grace, which communicates to that soul interior peace and joy.

∞

Oh, sublime City, send down your beams of Light to these regions of darkness, this shadow of death where we still miserably live. Come, oh Supernatural Light, to reveal to us the beauties of that Blessed Country, and detach us from the miseries of this earth; make our eyes so pure that, through the shining crystal of Faith, they may behold the eternal good which awaits us after a short time of sacrifice and self-conquering. He who fights will be victorious, and to the victor the prize is Heaven.

❦

Just as we were passing, a most beautifully coloured rainbow appeared in the sky which seemed to unite the inhabitants of the city with the passengers of the steamer. The rainbow seemed to announce the Peace of the Divine Heart which draws the hearts of all people together in ardent charity. Behind this arc there was a still larger and more extended rainbow with lighter tints; it was a sight which made us hold our breath. It looked like a heavenly light spread out to purify the mind and render it capable of raising itself to praise the Maker of Creation, so immense and enchanting and inimitable by man.

❦

Love the good God, for the sky, earth and sea tell us to love Him! The immense ocean, set with wonderful gems, reveals clearly the ineffable solicitude (with graces and blessings) with which our loving Creator surrounds us. We look at the sea, the earth with its inexhaustible fecundity, the firmament with its stars, and the whole Universe reflects God's attributes. His power. His wisdom and goodness, and we cannot but exclaim with admiration, "How wonderful is God in His works!"

Week 5

God's Creation

We had Heaven in our hearts. The immensity of the ocean, with its most clear and vast horizon, raises our minds to Heaven. It seems as if the sky, with its clouds of singular beauty, touches the waters of the ocean. All this helps to raise one's mind to the most beautiful contemplation, and seems to bring us to the door of Heaven, and to enable us to hear the echoes of those holy and sweet words which the Church repeats with great jubilee, "Alleluia, Alleluia." Holy Mother Church never tires of repeating these words, as though to give us here below a foretaste of the harmonies of Heaven.

∽

Yesterday the fog was obstinate, to-day it lifted at once, and we could see in this the figure of a docile soul which allows itself to be overcome by the grace of God, the Sun of Justice, whilst a rebellious soul resists all the most beautiful graces, and becomes hard and exposes itself to great danger.

∽

They are the work of the Immortal Artist, Whose existence men dare to deny and to forget while the powerful and wonderful works of His hands speak so eloquently.

Week 6

Conversion of Heart

To-day the skin has begun to peel off my forehead and nose. I am changing like a serpent. God wants me to change my life and be converted; to confirm this, my dearest daughters, pray. The Sacred Heart of Jesus will always hear favourably the prayers of children for their Mother. Pray! Pray! I am in need of your intercession. When I am converted and begin to lead a good life, it is certain that this will obtain many beautiful graces for the Institute. However, I am happy to think you have been so good. Continue to be good, more generous and sacrificing, humble and meek on all occasions, especially in the moments when you feel self-love.

The flames of human passions, which always leave a void and a sense of dissolution, become changed into celestial flames through grace, and the ... supernatural light of Heaven, once let into the soul, grows so wonderfully that the human passions become a volcano of Divine Love, a real fire that nobody can extinguish as long as goodwill remains in the soul.

And you, dear daughters, who are destined to continue the Mission of the Apostles, enter often into yourselves, amidst the retirement and silence which your rules allow. Look into your souls. See how you behave in moments of adversity and prosperity, both of which form the two storms of our lives. Greater is the storm of prosperity than that of adversity, but in either you may be shipwrecked.

∽

Examine yourselves well at the two examinations of conscience every day, which are exacted by your rule. See if you allow inordinate affections to predominate, and if you behave as you should when exposed to winds contrary to your spiritual welfare, no matter how much they serve to flatter your imagination and desires.

My Thoughts and Prayers

Week 7

Conversions at Sea

A Protestant gentleman last night came and asked me to go with all the Sisters to a concert. I told him we could not accept the invitation, as Religious did not go to secular entertainments or amusements. He wanted to stay with us. He presented us with six tickets of a lottery worth half-a-dollar each, and he promised to be on the alert when the tickets were being drawn. I am sorry I do not understand, as this gentleman is a very good man. I like his frankness and the manner in which he speaks of our Holy Religion. Patience! pray to the Sacred Heart and Our Lady for his salvation. He is an Englishman who has lived for five years in New York. He promised to come and bring his wife with him to see our Orphanage; his wife is a Catholic. This gentleman thinks we have undertaken a very difficult mission, which offers little probability of success—that of the Italians; but hearing that it was just for this reason we undertook it, and will at any cost work for it, he has more esteem for us than ever, and is willing to give us help.

∽

Yesterday we had a discussion, and he ended by saying I was right. He loves the Pope very much and feels a profound veneration for him. He also has a great esteem for our holy Religion, but he does not wish to embrace it because he has seen so many priests without the true spirit; but also on this point he understood well when I told him the reason. You should see with what patience he listens to me when I speak.

Also another passenger, a certain De Pedro, Milanese, is travelling with us. At first he did not make himself known as an Italian, but when he saw everybody coming to us and making friends, he came also and declared his friendship, saying how happy he was to know us. Now he delights in speaking Milanese with all his power. He admires also the success we have achieved in a few months, while he, for fifteen years, so he says, found nothing but sorrows and disappointments numerous enough to fill a volume. The poor man does not know Jesus and the goodness of His Heart. He trusts only to his talents. Thus his days cannot be happy.

Oh, let us pray, my daughters, let us pray for so many of our brethren, and let their blindness be a good lesson and teach us to be more faithful in the observance of our Holy Rules, in order to console the afflicted Heart of Jesus, and obtain from Him blessings in great abundance for ourselves and for our neighbours. Their mistake will induce us to remain very humble in order that we may be enlightened and never allow our intellect to be darkened. God resists and confounds the proud, whereas He reveals Himself to the humble, and draws them nearer to Him and caresses them.

My Thoughts and Prayers

Week 8

Love of God and the Gift of Grace

I don't feel ill, but I am not well, and I have no desire to do anything. Nevertheless I am in the happy position of being able to meditate freely. This is a great advantage for me, because I am able to pass the time conversing with the sweet Spouse of my soul.

⁓

Oh, if everyone had the knowledge of the great and beautiful advantages of meditation and of speaking familiarly with Jesus, if they could experience these heavenly joys, they would certainly envy our happy life (or state). Instead, how many poor creatures are there who do not want to know Him, in order to follow their own passions more freely, blinded by the smoke of the false pleasures of the world! In these circumstances, and at the sight of so many miserable and unfortunate creatures, how much better we are able to understand the great grace that God has given us by calling us to His Divine Service, or, to express it more accurately, to His love.

⁓

Let us love Jesus, then, my daughters, let us love Him very much. Jesus has ready for us many other graces, but He is waiting to be loved by us more and more, in order to grant these graces to us.

⁓

On one occasion He said to one of His faithful servants, that if he could find souls who would love Him, as Saint Francis of Assisi did, He would give as many graces as He bestowed upon that Saint, and even greater ones. Indeed, it is true. Let us confess it. If graces do not descend upon us, it is because of our little love of God, which keeps them back from us. And we shall never get a true love for God unless we try to overcome our self-love and the attachment to ourselves and our own judgment.

My Thoughts and Prayers

Week 9

The Missionary Vocation

If the Sacred Heart would give me the means I would construct a boat called "The House of Cristoforo" ("Bearer of Christ") to traverse with one Community, little or big, so as to carry the Name of Christ to all people, to those who as yet do not know Him, and also to those who have forgotten Him.

❧

Zeal is a great charity but only when it is tempered with great, kind and gentle love like that of the heart of Jesus. Gentle words move the heart of the most hardened souls and lead to repentance; I will try to be always gentle in my approach.

❧

When words have no effect let us have recourse to prayer, asking the heart of Jesus to touch the hearts of these persons. How much better than we ourselves can He accomplish this!

❧

Your love must be active as that of Jesus on Golgotha. "Sitio," "I thirst," cried Jesus, "for souls." If you love God, come forth, have courage, the devil laughs at the weak, at the timid, whereas he fears and flies from energetic souls.

❧

Are you fearful? She who trusts in God and mistrusts herself, need fear nothing, because stripped of herself and strong with the strength of God, and with faith and humility, she can defy everything. Mind, dangers only exist for those who put themselves in the way of them, who mix up the things of the world with the things of God. On the other hand, those who are untrammelled with the things of the world, seek God alone and His service, and His glory, run no risk.

My Thoughts and Prayers

Missionary Zeal

We are Missionaries, my daughters, we are Missionaries of the Divine Heart. If, then, we do not burn with love, we do not deserve to bear the beautiful title which ennobles us, elevates us, makes us great, and even a spectacle to the angels in Heaven.

⁓

For a Missionary, however difficult the voyage, it is always on that small plank that she must seek to extend the kingdom of love of Jesus. Therefore another four thousand miles is very little after all. You pray, and that will suffice. I will do the rest, giving myself up to the Heart of Jesus, He Who is our Good, our All, Our Preserver, our Master, Friend and Spouse.

⁓

Then once more we rowed amidst the waves, singing hymns of thanksgiving. Here again the birds hover over us, drawn there either by the hoarseness or sweetness of our voices, to adore and praise their Creator Whom we carried in our hearts as in living Tabernacles. Some of the Sisters wanted to know what this procession meant, and I replied that they represented the Religious of those countries who might enter our Institute some day, but one of the Sisters was not convinced of my interpretation, and answered, "They rather (as the birds were about a thousand in number) represent the souls that shall be saved by us." I still argued, when another flight of other aquatic birds appeared, a thousand or more, and eventually we decided that they represented the souls which were to be saved by us in the course of time.

∞

I would like to convert all Protestants. This is a mission I have very much at heart, and you, my dear daughters, by the duties of your holy vocation, find yourselves engaged in this sublime mission of converting souls. Do attend to it with great zeal and fervour, and try to multiply the grapes of the mystic vine of Christ. You should use every possible means and skill in order to succeed in converting souls, and be certain you will never be wanting in means and knowledge if you love your Celestial Spouse, because the love of Jesus suggests a thousand ways we may use for the interests of His glory.

∞

The Protestant lady never leaves us. She likes to stay with us. To-day I made her a present of a small cross, on which may be seen the picture of Our Lady. She thanked me so much for this cross, and said to me, "It may be that one day I shall be a Catholic!" Oh, daughters, pray that this may be so. How happy I should be if she entered the true fold of Holy Church. She is a lady who has much influence, and therefore how she would extend our Religion to many other souls. Let us pray. By prayer we can obtain everything.

My Thoughts and Prayers

Week 11

Missionary Work:
Sanctification and Trust

Oh, blessed voice of obedience! When that speaks, the Missionary crosses the ocean and gives no thought to the roaring waters, the rising and lowering of the billows, but the ocean becomes to her a sublime and magnificent sight that fills her with admiration, and induces her to praise the Creator for the beauty and wonder of His works.

Even here on board ladies and gentlemen approach us and tell us how necessary it is to have Missionaries in these parts who will work with true zeal for the good of the people. Oh! my God, bless our intentions, and give us zeal for the salvation of our neighbours' souls, and communicate to us that energy which knows no measure and overcomes all difficulties confiding in the Sacred Heart of Jesus.

Our great Patron, Saint Francis Xavier, said, "He who goes holy to the Missions will find many occasions to sanctify himself more, but he who goes poorly provided with holiness, runs the risk of losing what he has and of falling away." I become more convinced of this truth every day, and as experience is a great master, let us take advantage of the lessons it teaches and never let a day pass without examining our conscience and making serious resolutions to acquire the virtues we need.

Week 12

The Burning Charity
of the Missionary

We left Gibraltar yesterday, and, steering through the Straits, passed Spain, or had a glimpse of it; but we turned with sighs and groans towards Morocco, that poor land to which we would willingly fly to give succor to those poor souls which the Word of God has not as yet reached. It is true, vast crusades of Christ's Missionaries are already on this soil, but the land is vast, the ignorance extreme, and the help is insufficient. May Missionary Priests and Sisters multiply in numbers!

The harvest is great, the labourers are few! To you, Christian maidens, do I speak especially, love God, and make yourselves active with the zeal that burns in you; help your poor abandoned brethren, who are the price of the blood of Christ, join our band and try to give a large number of souls to the Heart of Jesus.

Oh, dear Jesus, what terrible ruin! But in Thy mercy turn not Thy face away from us. Arise, great Giant of Love, arise, O my Beloved! Come into the field of the Missions of Thy beloved Spouses, who desire to bring into Thy Kingdom every human soul. Come! We wait, desire and sigh for Thee. Come, refulgent Sun, with Thy bright and vivid rays, that they may brighten the earth enveloped in dense darkness!

O Jesus, the Desired of Ages, Love all on fire for Thy children, hasten and give life to those who are sitting in the darkness of death! Through Thy Most Holy Heart, heal the gaping, bleeding wounds of sick humanity! We, Thy Missionaries, turn our eyes and our hearts always towards Thy Divine Heart, and, if Thou willest, all those confided to our care will be saved. Yes, if Thou wish it, it can be done, for Thy very Name indicates salvation, grace, unction and love. The more I invoke Thy sweet name, the more I find it dear, sweet and amiable.

Thou art my life, my all, console then her who loves Thee, console Thy poor servant and save, yes, save this sick generation, which you have trusted to us. Look upon those souls whom Thou hast redeemed with Thy Precious Blood. Look upon them with love and mercy. Wound them with the darts of Thy burning charity, warm and transform all, in Thee.

My Thoughts and Prayers

The Missionary as the
Mystical Body of Christ

There was a time when Our Lord went through the streets of Jerusalem drawing souls to Himself by His Divine looks; but, to-day, it is by His spirit and His loving Heart that He draws souls to His following and inflames them. My Jesus, how good Thou art! I shall never cease to speak of Thee and Thy Divine Heart! I shall never tire of proclaiming Thy praises, so that Thou risest every day like a bright and ardent lamp and run as a Giant in every country, enlightening souls, warming up hearts, drawing them into the fold of Thy Church and helping them to follow Thee more closely.

Pray, dear daughters, pray much for the conversion of England. It breaks one's heart that this country does not possess the true Faith. England has all the qualities that make it worthy to be a portion of Christ's fold. Her only fault is that of having but half of the Faith, and no longer being allied with the only Head which forms the perfect union of the Church with Christ. Our Lord Himself said so: "He who does not enter by the door of the fold shall not have salvation." The door of the fold is the Catholic Church and union with the Head who represents Jesus Christ. It is faith in Christ, a pure, simple faith, not half a faith, but entire faith, that faith which embraces in its universality the revealed Word of God, which is necessary to enter the true Church. Such a faith makes us living members of the mystic Body of the Redeemer. In fact, of what avail is it, children, if Protestants lead naturally pure, honest lives, yet possess virtues which lack the interior impulse of the Holy Ghost? They may well say "We do no harm, we lead good lives"; but, if they do not enter the true fold of Christ, all their protestations are in vain, because a really good life is that which is so formed and ordered as to lead to the Way that is Blessed and Eternal. Without this admirable order and relationship a good life is of no value. These poor people do not enter the door of the true fold of Christ, because they do not know Christ perfectly, or, at least, do not accept in their entirety His Sacred Commands.

Let us open wide our hearts, let us help those souls lying under the yoke of the king of darkness. Let us break, by the fire of ardent Charity, the heavy chains that bind these poor souls to the terrible slavery of the devil, and we shall see that our efforts are not in vain.

My Thoughts and Prayers

Week 14

The Missionary of the Sacred Heart, in Imitation of Christ

Let us imagine we are like Saint Francis Xavier, and always keep our Divine Lord before us, beholding His mild gravity, His quiet amiability, His unalterable evenness of temper. In thus copying his Divine Model, we shall see how he worked, walked, spoke, and taught. Let us think of the perfection that accompanied every act, and let us force ourselves to imitate Him at all times and in every moment with the fidelity which is possible to us.

The days fly, souls are being lost. Death is approaching more quickly than we realize, and then the time for work is over.

Work, then, while you have time. Work with energy, and especially with the spirit of sacrifice, for it is this that forms the true Missionary. This storms the Heart of Jesus, and draws from It, as it were, the most precious graces for those souls who are the hardest and the most obstinate in resisting His love. Work with an apostolic spirit which offers everything, actions, prayers and sacrifices for the conversion of souls.

Seek amongst your acquaintances, above all, among those who wish to do some good for the glory of God, souls who will co-operate with us and give material help for our Missions. Saint Paul, in one of his letters to the Philippians, speaks of his predilection towards those who are generous and help with their offerings, and he calls them co-workers of the Gospel.

How many beautiful souls there are in the world whose hearts are filled with zeal and with the love of God, and who are distressed at the thought of so many about to be lost. They wish to do something to save souls. Not being able, on account of their position, to consecrate themselves to this great Apostolic work, they timidly keep repeating to themselves, "Oh, if I could do something for those souls," and they proceed no further. Teach them that, without leaving or neglecting the obligations of their state or country, they can become Missionaries of the Sacred Heart, and that they will find themselves among the number of those who enter Heaven followed by a number of souls saved by them. But how? you will ask.

The first condition is prayer. Saint Teresa helped the great apostle of the Indies, Saint Francis Xavier, by praying and sacrificing herself in the solitude of her cell. The second condition is to help the Missions entrusted to the Institute by offerings. God's judgments are very different from the judgments of the world. The world judges from appearance, and gives honour and glory to those who do not merit them. God sees everything, even our most sacred thoughts, and knows how to trace the origin of that small offering which did so much good, and which therefore may have been the first and real author of the good done by the Missionaries of the Sacred Heart in far-distant lands.

What is given to the Missionary is given to God, because given for the benefit of the poor and the abandoned. If it is sweet to deprive oneself in order to give, how much more consoling, is it not, to give to God from Whom we have received everything? He will not allow Himself to be outdone in generosity. He who is so good and magnificent! Banks fail, thieves steal, the moth destroys, storms ruin possessions, but the money given to God is placed in the Divine Treasury, where it repays a hundredfold.

Week 15

The Missionary and
the Gift of Faith

The Colonel came on deck accompanied by the Doctor
and other persons and begged us to sing some of the
little hymns they heard us sing a few days before. So
we sang, in chorus, "Gesù mio ver conforto" ("Jesus,
my true comfort") and then "Maria, che dolci affetti"
("Mary, what sweet affection"), and our voices, blending
with the sound of the waves, were raised to Heaven,
while the listeners' faces brightened up with a new
pleasure, which, perhaps, some never enjoyed before.
It was Jesus and Mary who were passing their celestial
rays over these souls, for whom we were secretly praying that they might be given the precious gift of faith.

Let the Blessed Virgin be honoured in these countries
of palms and flowers, which are an image of her, and
may there be a perfect and complete conversion of all
these souls.

Poor souls! These are they for whom Christ shed so
much Blood, who so much grieved His Heart in His
sorrowful agony when He saw, in all the horror of His
imminent Passion, the uselessness of His agony for so
many souls. Oh, how bitter to the Sacred Heart was
such a thought! How painful those stripes, thorns and
nails of the Cross! If it were only possible for us to console the Divine Heart, to comfort Him, and to become
victims for the salvation of souls that cost such a dear

price! Such comfort we can give to Jesus. All of us can devote ourselves to this enterprise by means of prayer.

⁘

Let us be generous in our little sacrifices to Our Lord for the success of Catholic Missions. Perhaps, one day, when we ourselves are gathered into the Eternal Tabernacle, we shall meet many souls who will tell us that they owe their eternal happiness to us.

My Thoughts and Prayers

Week 16

The Religious Vocation: Spouses of the King

Worldlings look with esteem on Religious who despise the pleasures of the world; they revere them and will have recourse to them in their needs. What an honour Christian maidens, if God calls you to extend His Kingdom! Let us be up and doing! Do not refuse and incur the rebuke given to the Foolish Virgins, by neglecting to take advantage of the opportunity which the Institute affords us of co-operating in saving souls, and thus gaining merits, which in Heaven will fructify in an immeasurable reward of glory.

Virgins are chosen Spouses of the King and therefore Queens. If they are Queens, they must have a people over whom to exercise their power—their celestial Mission of Peace. Just as the Virgin, working as a Missionary, gains souls to Christ, so she extends her dominions, and her scepter becomes more powerful and more glorious.

Come, prudent Virgins, and enlarge the Missionary Army, come, and make all nations give one another the kiss of peace. Come, for the Kingdom of God has no limits; its limits are those of the globe itself. Come, and let your glory be the glory of your celestial Spouse, the working out of that celestial talent—the sublime vocation of co-operating with Christ for the salvation of souls. Come, for in the Vineyard of the Great Father of the family we are to gather rich and copious sheaves. There are some who may think they are too poor, ignorant and weak to undertake such work. Do not fear, mistrust yourselves and confide in God, for, as I have already said, "Omnia possum in Eo qui me confortat." "With God I can do all things."

∞

He who calls us is that same Jesus who said, "Be perfect even as your Heavenly Father is perfect." But how are we to attain such perfection? By the grace of Him Who deigns to impose such an injunction upon us. When the Virgin of Christ mistrusts herself and confides completely in Jesus Christ, she can do all things. She becomes powerful, and can at every instant repeat, "With God I shall do great things."

∞

To this beautiful soul consecrated to God, every sign from Jesus is invaluable. Such a Religious not only performs what is hourly prescribed for her, but joyfully anticipates His every desire. She no longer lives for herself but for her Beloved; she has, as it were, wings to fly wherever the Divine will calls her, and to do and suffer something for Jesus.

My Thoughts and Prayers

Week 17

The Missionary as Consoler of the Divine Heart

You, the chosen portions of Christ's flock, are destined to console His Divine Heart; you, who by your work, prayers and obedience, can procure the glory of that Heart, have become by your precious vocation the chosen portion of my heart.

∾

The conversion of sinners and the sanctification of souls does not depend on sterile cold human eloquence, or the grace of style and flowery rhetoric, but on the fructifying grace of Jesus Christ. Jesus alone can give life to words and arguments. He enlightens the mind, moves the will, sows virtue, and animates us to undertake holy and perfect works.

∾

How pleasing it is to the Holy Ghost to see zealous souls that seek to spread the Kingdom of Jesus Christ! We give Divine homage when we convert a sinner, or make known more clearly and more distinctly the knowledge of Jesus Christ. Work, work indefatigably, without tiring, for the salvation of souls.

∾

May the Holy Spirit work in you, pray with you and communicate to you His lights, graces and treasures. If you are zealous, He will really enlighten you with His Divine Light. He will assist you in your works and trials. He will support you in danger, defend you from internal and external enemies, and strengthen you by His virtue. Have faith, great faith; faith and confidence, and pray constantly. The Holy Spirit, with His immense Charity, will then diffuse Himself into your hearts and in your souls in order to make them stronger with His own fortitude. "Ignem veni mittere in terram, et quid volo nisi ut accendatur?"

My Thoughts and Prayers

Week 18

The Missionary's Apostolic Vocation

And you, my dear daughters, I leave you in the Heart of Jesus, where we must remain united together, though we are four or six thousand miles apart. The Missionary knows no distance—the world is so small. Space is an imperceptible object to a Missionary, because she is accustomed to dwell on eternity, to which she wishes to conduct all the souls she can—those souls which have been redeemed by the Most Precious Blood of Jesus Christ.

"You are the light of the world, the salt of the earth," Jesus said, when from the mountain He spoke to His Apostles. And you, Missionaries of the Sacred Heart, belong in a certain measure to the Apostolic family. Have you not to continue the Apostolate of the great Mission of Christ? To you also is entrusted the Mission of being the salt of the earth and the light of the world.

Reflecting upon my vocation as a Missionary, I remembered that I ought not to allow sadness to take hold of me. So I entered into the Heart of Jesus, where I saw all the Sisters, and though I could not speak to them, I asked the Sacred Heart to tell each of them what I had forgotten, or what I had not time to say. Great was my pleasure at the thought that the Sacred Heart would inspire you with the good resolution to do what I want you to do, and to add to it His Grace, and thus facilitate the exercise of those virtues which give to true

Missionaries of the Sacred Heart that energy which makes them zealous for the salvation of souls.

∞

Vast and fruitful is the harvest that the good God spreads out before you, and you can extend your zeal all over it, gathering every day abundant sheaves. You are the fortunate Spouses of Jesus; you are therefore made the queens of all the treasures of the King. Keep in mind that souls were redeemed by the Blood of Jesus, and therefore you must do all in your power to lead them to the Divine Heart. Work with fervour. Love will enable you to work with fervour and fruit. In your actions, your words and your sufferings, seek always the greater glory of God, and even perfection to which you must incessantly aspire will be animated by that most noble end—the glory of God. Unite all the powers of your spirit; work, pray and suffer.

∞

Do continual violence to yourselves, ever mindful of the words, "Omnia possum in Eo qui me confortat." Have great confidence in God; let your confidence grow greater every day. You are poor creatures, and so you must lean on the Creator. You are weak and miserable, hence you must rely on the Divine Omnipotence. Yes, my daughters, lean on your Beloved, because the soul that abandons itself to the Most Adorable Heart of Jesus in everything it does, is not only sustained but even carried forward by Jesus Himself.

My Thoughts and Prayers

Week 19

Missionaries, the Angels of the Earth

Remember, daughters, you are the tutelary Angels of the earth, therefore you should always be ready when holy obedience calls, to fly over the vast fields which charity lays before you. Let your lives be a perennial sacrifice of yourselves in behalf of the human race. Let your joy consist in working much and praying much.

Always renew your offering as victims of expiation and reconciliation between Heaven and earth. In contradictions and difficulties, bear in mind how Our Lord let the Apostles work all night in vain, midst the storm to try them, so that they might accustom themselves to suffer adversity, and not grow faint in the midst of persecutions they would meet in the course of their lives, but, rather, resist and go forward whatsoever the difficulty might be.

She who consecrates herself to Jesus as a Missionary Sister, willing to carry His name even to the utmost ends of the earth, sacrificing her dearest affection and even life itself, is a true heroine in whose heart the flame of love burns brightly. She does not stifle her own heart nor put under a bushel the shining light of intelligence with which God has endowed her. On the contrary, the flame kindled in her heart becomes a regular volcano of love which embraces everything. That gleam of light becomes a brilliant torch, causing darkness to disappear and erring souls to find their way. Happy the one who, at the tribunal of God, will be able to present herself followed by a great number of souls saved through her.

My Thoughts and Prayers

Week 20

The Church in the Fallen World

For, unfortunately, [the passengers] have amongst them a rabid anarchist, who often gathers them around him and, like Belial, incites them to revolt against authority and order in such a manner that the officers of the boat have to interfere. This is a small picture of many European nations, whose sons have lost the true sense of patriotism, at the mercy of their disorderly passions and of civil wars. They go rapidly towards their last ruin, the just punishment of God upon those who have forgotten that the Catholic Religion of their country constitutes their principal nobility and security.

Sister Bernardina is going to make a novena for me to obtain the grace to speak English, and assures me she will obtain it. What do you think of it? I fear the day of judgment will arrive before I learn English. Notwithstanding, I trust in my good Jesus, and if He wants me to bring to His Heart any souls, He will also give me the grace to speak the language of the country I shall visit.

A Freemason, who, as soon as he saw two Sisters on board the ship, made enquiries and then telegraphed to the Police to prevent our entering the country. To-day everyone is looking down upon him for acting so inhumanly towards two ladies. The more sensible minds are doing all they can to obtain a permit for us to visit any part of the Republic we wish, so as not to let us leave the country with such an unfavourable impression. I told them it would now be useless, as we were leaving for our destination soon.

∽

Here, however, we were able to perform our little devotions, even closing the month of May in a small country church, which is kept very nicely by the parish priest, who is a member of the Mission of Saint Vincent de Paul.

My Thoughts and Prayers

Week 21

The Temptations of
the Modern World

The devil has placed his throne very comfortably there and extends his net in thick darkness, as seen once by Saint Anthony, and he really catches a great many fish without much trouble, because to these poor things the word "progress" is like a siren, which allures them and offers them the hidden poison which leads them backwards instead of forwards.

See how dangerous these times are to our faith, to our august religion and to sound morals, for the emissaries of Satan, violent apostles of unrestrained liberty and freedom of speech, make use of all kinds of opportunities and snares, and go not only into the towns, but even into remote villages to spread their errors and doctrines, which are, as you know, condemned by the Church. It seems as if all the diabolical powers of hell have combined in directing their satanic efforts to combat and persecute the Church, her doctrines and her morals, her laws, her worship, her ministers, and all that she possesses of holiness and reverence. In the meantime, the weak, lukewarm, incautious, drink in the venomous errors, the fatal maxims of which pervert the mind and corrupt the heart, miserably dragging innumerable souls to eternal perdition. One cannot but grieve over this terrible war which the demon never ceases to rage against our holy Religion. One trembles for the frightful future that awaits the world if God does not show an efficacious way out, which must be something out of the ordinary, as the evils that are now affecting the Church are extraordinary.

We have occasion to feel great sorrow in seeing men who, after abandoning the Catholic Religion, after having rebelled against Jesus Christ, reach the precipice of Atheism, Pantheism and Materialism. "There is no God," the first say. "There is no difference between good and evil," the second say. "There is nothing better than to accumulate riches by all possible means, and to give way to pleasure," exclaim the last. By means of these insensate theories they have upset the world, and many have lost their own good sense and reason. From such errors have come all the misfortunes that affect the present and menace the future.

Oh, daughters, let us render the homage of our fidelity and love to our most loving Jesus, Who with ineffable mercy has deigned to enrich us with all that is necessary to obtain our temporal and eternal felicity. We are the children of God. Let us try not to degenerate from such a high and sublime dignity, and let us see that our heart, our soul and our life be always and entirely consecrated to this merciful and good Father. Let us pray that we and all creatures may give glory to God in time and eternity, that His most holy law may reign and govern us and all men from one end of the Universe to the other.

My Thoughts and Prayers

Week 22

Sanctifying the Fallen World

The world is poisoned with erroneous theories, and needs to be taught sane doctrines, but it is difficult to straighten what has become crooked. It is in your hands to form new generations, to lead them in the right direction, to instil into them those principles which are the seed of good works, though for the moment they may seem hidden. The impressions of childhood are never obliterated. We shall be indebted to you, if the youth whom you educate, when grown up, become the pride of the family, of Society, of the State, and, especially, the honour and support of our Holy Faith.

Our good God, who, as the child recites in the catechism, has created Heaven and earth, is almost banished from the world—there is no place for Him. Man has made an idol of himself which he adores, and so does not pray to, or adore, the true and only God. No wonder, then, that after superhuman efforts, nature, weak and impotent to fight any longer, or to attain what it seeks, abandons itself to despair, suicide and crime. Prayer would have obviated all this. Prayer is like an incense rising to Heaven, and draws exhilarating graces from Heaven. It strengthens the strayed soul, giving it back peace and calm.

Oh, if the voice of religion at least could reach all these poor people, and teach them to make holy and noble such fatiguing work, and to render it fruitful for Eternity, what a boon it would be for them! Thus you see the tremendous responsibility resting on those who take away the gift of faith from the working classes, for in so doing they rob them of every hope of the future life, banishing the love of God from their hearts. Take away the supernatural principles and dictates of our Holy Faith, and what remains but wickedness and the indulgence of every passion?

Pray, my good daughters, that the number of Missionary workers may be increased, and that they may be really zealous and goodhearted, because the efforts of such are capable of arresting the materialism and unbelief which, like a most subtle ether, infiltrates itself everywhere, causing great, immense and irreparable damage.

My Thoughts and Prayers

Week 23

Omnia in Christo

Pray that all the docile Faithful may listen to the voice of the Vicar of Jesus Christ, Pope Pius X, who, conscious of these great evils which threaten to shake the foundations of Society, proposes to restore everything in Christ. Strong in the strength of God, assisted as he is by the Holy Ghost, he will not fail to fulfil in the Church the high mission to which God has elected him, but at the same time what fatigue he must suffer, what cares, what troubles must torment his heart, and preoccupy his mind in such an arduous task. At least let him feel that he is comforted by the love and obedience of his children, and let him find in each and everyone that co-operation which it is our bounden duty to give to him. This co-operation will make possible the fulfilment of the holy designs of the Pope and the arresting of the many evils which threaten to overwhelm the world.

∽

Take religion away from man, and nothing remains in this life but illusion, trials and afflictions without number. Where can he find the strength to resign himself to trials and misfortune, if he has not the comforting thoughts which religion suggests? Whence do rebellions and seditions arise, if not from a lack of religion? We are greatly mistaken if, desirous as each one is in her own sphere to contribute to the greatness of our country, we do not base our hopes on that corner stone which is Christ and His Church.

∽

In union with Your painful agony in the Garden, I offer myself for all those in their last agony all over the world at every hour so that they may repent and die in Your loving embrace.

My Thoughts and Prayers

Week 24

Spiritual Communion

Yesterday, the 21st, we desired to pay a return visit to Panama, but the passage cost too much so we satisfied our desire for Holy Communion by the thought of having received Our Lord the day before and by drawing Him into the Mystic Tabernacle of our hearts through Spiritual Communion.

It is only one day since I received Jesus in my heart, and I imagine He is still there. One remembers Jacob's mystical dream when he saw a mystic ladder and angels descending and ascending, who revealed many mysteries and secrets to Jacob and assured him and his descendants of God's protection. Though we are far from the Holy Tabernacle, still even here on the sea there is a mystic ladder which touches Heaven, and the angels ascend and descend upon it for us also. From its summit God looks down upon us and makes generous promises. We can, therefore, repeat with Jacob, "Really, God is here in this place and we did not know it."

We are in the bosom of the Catholic Church. We always lay our heads on the dear and mystic stone of Jesus; we agree with Him in everything, and abandon ourselves to Him, tranquil and secure, and by thus doing we merit in Jesus and by Jesus to partake of the good and the graces He brings us. Jesus is looking at me from the summit of the ladder; I invite Him to come to me spiritually, and He descends at once into my heart.

∽

So, here again on this voyage we are deprived of Holy Mass and Holy Communion. But, after all, God wishes it thus, so let us cherish the memory of the last reception of Him, as Holy Viaticum, in Genoa. As I have said before, He helps, consoles and comforts us. We are representing the fifteen mysteries, and God, in His immense goodness, leaves us to enjoy Him. He is our Paradise—the Heaven of our desires.

∽

The heavens were so clouded that I could not distinguish the points of the compass, which might have helped me to look in the proper direction. I then looked into the Sacred Heart, where I could see you in deep contemplation like so many inflamed seraphim in preparation for Holy Communion. It was a most consoling vision for me, and I hastened to unite myself with you in Spiritual Communion, offering it to the Eternal Father in union with your Sacramental Communion.

My Thoughts and Prayers

Week 25

Separation and Death

I never felt the bitterness of the separation so much as at this time, my beloved daughters, when saying "Au revoir in Heaven," in the name of those of your Sisters who perhaps you may never see again. It seemed to me I had said it also for myself, though I don't feel that I shall die yet. What human weakness! What kind of missionary spirit is this, you will say to me. It is true; you are right; no matter how great the distance that separates us, we are always near to each other, because we are ever found in the little space of this world, which to our small and narrow minds sometimes seems so big.

Fresh water and salty water mixed together form a calm sea, and this lesson teaches us how to behave with those who are against us. Raise your hearts on high and accept God's will without murmuring against or criticising those people who afflict us. Pity them and excuse them as did David with regard to his enemy, for, on hearing himself reviled, he did not defend himself, but said, "Let them talk, because it is God who permits their speaking against me; it is little, indeed, they are saying, I merit more." Thus behaves a soul according to the Heart of God. If we become possessors of such virtues, we would become Saints very easily.

Week 26

The Science of Suffering

As long as we remain faithful to our vocation, Jesus will always be in the midst of us, inflaming our hearts with Divine Love. He will try our faith and our love sometimes, by allowing us to be tempted and tried, but, if we are faithful to our vows, and if, trustingly, we invoke Him, not forgetting that the Fount of every good is in our midst. He will soon console us and leave us flooded with His light and celestial joy. He will always be with us in the time of our trials. He will walk by our side and help us out of all difficulties. He Himself has called us to follow Him closely, and has promised to help us; surely. He will keep His word.

~

We may have to suffer a long time on the road to the Mount of Perfection, but we should not be frightened, for, what does she, who ignores Christian suffering, know of what is grand and wonderful? The science of suffering is the science of the Saints. Let us rejoice when an unexpected cross visits us, when a sorrow afflicts us, because these are the precious fruits of the mystical vine, destined to produce inestimable merits unto Eternity. Then, when you have suffered, dear daughters, do not go round sighing, as one who knows not the privilege of the Cross, but raise your eyes and smile sweetly at suffering, which is like a beautiful country white for the harvest. She who knows how to gather copious sheaves will receive a large reward.

~

Learn how to unite your sufferings sweetly with those of Jesus Christ, and, then, your sufferings endured for Jesus and for His Adorable Heart, will be as so many drops immersed in the immense ocean of the Most Holy Passion of Jesus Christ. In like manner, our trials and our sorrows offered up with those of our most loving Jesus, will be not only sanctified but made Divine and worthy of Eternal glory.

～

In suffering for Jesus we partake of His sufferings and riches, so that, during our earthly pilgrimage, grace will never be wanting, either to ourselves particularly or to the works of our mission — the salvation of souls. Be wise, then, dear daughters, and do not squander your sufferings, but submit to them without murmuring and with supernatural motives, remembering that in every sorrow a wonderfully secret work of grace is revolving within the wheels of our predestination.

～

Yes, yes, loveable Jesus, grant that I may keep you company here in the Garden of Olives in place of the disciples who sleep! My Jesus, I long to embrace you, to hold you close to my breast, while I wipe the precious drops of blood which inspire me with hope of salvation and the height of perfection!

～

Lord, unite me intimately with you. My love, Heart of my heart, Life of my life, loveable and tender sweetness of my soul, grant that I may never be separated from you! As you have inspired me, my Lord Jesus, and have long desired of me, behold I offer myself to you today and for all the rest of my life as a victim.

Week 27

Redemptive Suffering

I will not distinguish between suffering and suffering, nor why it comes from one source rather than from another. Any suffering will serve as a treasured means of reparation for my infidelities and an expression of love dear to Jesus. I will offer every pain with the intention of removing a thorn from the loving heart of Jesus and for the salvation of some soul for his greater glory.

Persecutions will never be lacking. The more I encounter them, the more I advance in the way of the spirit, the way of Christ who was persecuted throughout his life on earth.

Outwardly I will not show any signs of my interior sufferings but, according to the rule, I will always show cheerfulness in order to build up the community.

All for Jesus, all with Jesus, all in Jesus and for his most loving heart in which I desire to melt and lose myself.

I am created by God, I must live for God, with God, and only for his glory. How shall I glorify God? By depending entirely on his will. Therefore, a perfect indifference in all that God permits in me and about me. I will try to acquire a perfect equilibrium of spirit, not leaning more to one side then [*sic*] to the other, always praising God for whatever he permits.

∾

I will try never to complain, because all that God permits is only for my good. I will always maintain a pleasant expression, never permitting sadness for any happening, happy that God is pleased and not my ego. The ego I will crush.

∾

In the heart where the perfect love of God enters, no sin will ever enter. It is impossible to love God and sin, to so disgust him under his loving eyes. O my Jesus, how dear and loveable you are. Help me so that I may never offend you, whether for good or evil.

∾

The sacrament of Penance is one of the greatest gifts of the mercy of God. Have I always thought of it in this manner? How many times have I approached this sacrament coldly, without that lively faith and firm hope that cheers the soul and renders it capable of greater love of God?

∾

The sacrament of Penance is one of the greatest treasures for humility that we have to manifest to God our weaknesses. How precious is our humbling ourselves before him. An act of humility is better than the practice of the most showy virtue. Humility is truth and puts us in our proper place—in fact, what are we before God?

Week 28

Mary, the First Tabernacle

Mary is most holy, the meek dove of God in this universal deluge of corruption which frightens and depresses us. Mary with the flowery branch of the olive appears in our midst and seeks to give us hope. Adorned with that ineffable beauty of original innocence, she infuses in us great confidence, and makes us feel sweetly that she will present herself before God and obtain for us mercy and salvation.

～

What an admirable model we have in Mary. She is not yet three years old, and yet she abandons father, mother, country and friends, everything, indeed, and flies to God with the swift wings of a dove. She takes refuge in the Temple, a figure of our convents. She, this privileged Virgin, accomplishes, in the Temple of God, all that from her birth she had vowed to God. Mary sees herself rich in grace, fears nothing, and still she flees from the world and retires. Her profound humility is like a thick veil which she uses to hide herself and her gifts. She seeks solitude and silence, the solitary dove, because she desires to unite herself intimately with Him Who is Her only love. Mary will certainly have exclaimed, "How beautiful are Thy tabernacles!"

～

My God, may all souls burn and languish for Thee! My spirit and flesh are in Thee, O, my God, and my life! O, my God, Thou art my inheritance. Thou art my glory, my joy, my crown! How promptly Mary answered the Divine call, and we? How have we corresponded with the call of God? How do we correspond with the grace of God now? What is our virtue, our conduct? What are our efforts, our generosity?

∞

Mary knew her mission, and accomplished it. And what do we do? We also understand what our mission is, obedience shows the way, but do we follow it faithfully? Perhaps we allow ourselves to be carried away by self-love, our corrupted nature, human respect, pride, tepidity. O, daughters, do not lose time. Let us follow faithfully the footsteps of Mary, our sweet Mother. Let us conquer ourselves, cost what it may, and we shall have joy in our hearts and peace in our souls!

∞

Let us strive, O daughters, to conquer ourselves, and Mary will cover us with her mantle of virtues; then we shall not feel any trouble in making our journey. Let humility, daughters, humility and great charity, detachment from everything, from ourselves, accompany us everywhere.

∞

All the glory of the King's daughter is within. Of her preciously embroidered dress, of her immense riches, we see but the fringe. In Heaven, prayer will be explained in all its pomp and majesty. Pray, then, daughters, pray with unlimited faith in every need, in every difficulty, and do not become weary if in our short lives we do not see the effects of our prayers.

Have faith, lively faith, resting always assured that not one of our supplications will be rejected. Oh, faith! how beautiful, great, powerful! Faith produces hope, and prayer is at once the supplicating hope.

Week 29

Mary, Our Celestial Mother

Oh, how good is Mary! How sweet and amiable. The earth is full of her goodness. All the centuries have witnessed the wonderful and merciful works of her blessed hands. Do we not frequently experience how she evidently loves and protects us? Like a mother full of compassion for each one of us, she pitied us who, in our danger, invoked her with faith. Oh, what joy to be children of such a Mother! We shall always recall the wonders of her love!

∞

This morning the rainbow reminded me of our celestial Mother, the real Ark, who guides our little company across the sea. Mary is heavenly, and in her loveliness and serenity reflects the rays of the Divinity. She is a shining dart burning and inflamed with charity for us, because the splendours which are in her descend from God, Who is not only an ineffable light but a burning fire of charity. How many wonders we meet with in the love of Mary; how many graces, how many gifts, how many good things come from her benevolent hands, and all are sealed with great love. One look from her, one thought from her fills us with her burning charity.

∞

Mary, our sweet Mother, is an ocean of goodness, a fire of charity that burns, in flames and transforms. She is a sun of perennial light, grace and beneficence. No one is excluded from her beneficial heat, for her charity is universal and continual. To all she opens the bosom of her ineffable goodness; she is ready to help all, and even anticipates their desires.

Mary is like the beautiful olive tree in a field where all can see her and have access to her. From her fields flow perennial streams of water wherein the thirsty may quench their thirst. Do not wonder if you see yourselves overloaded with graces and tenderness from Mary, for she dispenses gifts and graces which flow like a stream from that immeasurable ocean of love she bears us.

As a cloud brightened by the rays of the sun becomes beautifully bright, so does Mary, the perfect image of Jesus, appear brilliant in her Divine Beauty.

Sweet mother, you are the dear and desired shoot of Jesse on whom I lean with profound humility and great confidence. Hear my plea to keep that beautiful flower, my beloved Jesus, so close to me that I will not even waste a leaf by being unfaithful.

I will study all ways to maintain the unity of holy charity with the sisters. I will love them with the heart of a true mother, trying to be the servant of all with respectful affection, seeing in each one the image of my beloved Jesus and the Virgin Mary.

Week 30

Mary, the Ladder
to Heaven

Mary is the Mysterious Book of Predestination to glory; she is lovable, love her. She is sublime and glorious, praise her. She is benign and merciful, appeal to her. Mary is your Mother, Mistress and Foundress, obey and fulfil her desires.

∽

Mary speaks to you plainly; listen to her, trust her with all your affections, she will alienate them from creatures, and you, as angelic spirits, will take refuge in the Heart of Jesus. Offer yourselves often to Mary, pray, work, suffer, recreate yourselves, rest and walk with Mary and beneath the gaze of Mary, and never sadden her in the least.

∽

She is dressed in blue and white, with rose-coloured lips, and carries an angelic smile, that diffuses silver rays which convince and inspire confidence and illuminate without injuring the eyes, despite their brilliancy. She is as white as the snow in her immaculate purity; she is heavenly in her grace and demeanour, all celestial in her majesty as Queen of Heaven, in her nobleness of mind and in the magnanimity of her thoughts. She is silver by reason of the rays of light which emanate from the heroic virtues she practised, which form a halo around her head and render her face shining and majestic....

∽

And the help needed to imitate our Holy Mother Mary is to be found in herself, if with great faith we place ourselves under her mantle of protection. If you find Mary, you find all. "Inventa Maria inveniuntur omnia bona, ipsa enim diligit diligentes se, imo sibi servientibus servit."

Oh, the greatness of Mary! She has been constituted the fount of all graces, the sure channel of Divine mercy, the ladder to Heaven, the gate of Paradise.

My Thoughts and Prayers

Week 31

Mary, Patroness of Missionaries

The Areopagite spoke well, when, after the Ascension of Our Lord, he pictured Our Lady as a Missionary encouraging and consoling the devout faithful: "If I had not known there was only one true Lord and God, I should have prostrated and adored Holy Mary as a Divinity."

❧

How beautiful it is to see souls who, like doves, fly over the earth, shedding over it their benign influence without being caught in the snares of the world. They fly, as it were, with always fresh zest, anxious to do good even when physical strength is wanting. They fly without tiring, or, rather, without being conscious of fatigue, until their works are surrounded by a halo of light, while their beneficent influence is always of great good because they are blessed by God.

❧

Mary, O children, is that mystical holy mountain, that mountain adorned by the Holy Ghost, that mountain from the summit of which springs the source of the clearest water, dividing itself into infinite streams which water the whole world. Therefore, our Houses, our works, are absolutely secure in the hands of Mary, as long as we show her faith, invoke her and imitate her virtues, as true Missionaries should do.

❧

If you desire to convert the whole world, invoke Mary, for she is that bright cloud, as seen by the prophet Elias, rising from the sea, gradually spreading over the whole heavens, and then breaking into rainfalls on every part of the earth, so that it covers even the remotest inhabitants of the globe.

∽

Yes, you can do everything with Mary. She extirpates heresy, eradicates schisms and destroys idols. She causes our Holy Faith to triumph everywhere, and increases and spreads the Fold of Christ which her mystic waters irrigate and fructify. Confide everything to her, then; do everything under her auspices, and do not leave her for one moment. Invoke her always, and she will cleanse your hearts and make them worthy of your high vocation.

∽

In order to be faithful and constant in Divine Love, let us try to remain always under the mantle of our most tender Mother. She is the Dove of Paradise, and in her conception crushed the head of our infernal and deceitful enemy. Look upon Mary and imitate her. Having corresponded faithfully with grace, she arrived at such a sublime degree of perfection, that she became the most wonderful prodigy of celestial virtue, and surpassed in sanctity all the Angels and Saints.

∽

Oh! dear Mother, on this beautiful day you seem to show forth in a most particular manner your beauty, your purity and your sanctity. Turn towards us your most loving eyes, which give joy to Heaven and consolation to the earth.

Shower upon us thy blessings, the most beautiful flowers of thy most precious virtues, that, under thy protection, thy children may preserve themselves and grow beautiful, odoriferous with celestial perfume, and merit to be one day transplanted into Heaven, where they will be with thee a pleasing incense to the most holy Heart of Jesus.

Week 32

Mary, the Morning Star

How beautiful is Mary! How amiable is this most noble creature! She is the manifestation of God on earth. Through her God will be known, adored, loved and blessed in the world, and so, rightly and in a special manner, Mary is the Mother of the Missionary of the Sacred Heart, who has for her scope the sublime mission of instructing her people in the knowledge and love of our Divine Redeemer, who, in the infinite goodness of His Divine Heart has deigned to call us to so sublime a vocation.

❧

Oh, how good and amiable is Mary! She is a propitious Morning Star; she is the inspiring guide of all our enterprises, and for this reason the Missionary Sisters of the Sacred Heart should fear nothing. Our great Mother and Foundress is near God, even united with God. Hence, she can do all, wish all, obtain all from God.

❧

What shall we fear, daughters, if Mary Immaculate, the pure Dove of God, is our Mother, our Refuge, our Hope, the cause of our joy? In God, dear daughters, let us put all our strength, our hope, as in their Principal Cause; in Mary as in their secondary cause. In God, as the prime cause of all good, of all graces. In Mary, as the salutary aqueduct through which we derive the most pure waters of His Divine Goodness and Mercy....

❧

She is, indeed, a singular Virgin, the Co-Redemptrix of the human race, the true Mother of the living. In Mary everything is great, providential: the mission of Mary in the world has a character all its own. She is like a resplendent sun, her light is immensely powerful, her splendour is heavenly, her beauty is divine.

∽

Mary lived more in God than in herself. She was more where she loved than where she lived, and therefore her intellect was more limpid and clear than those of the Seraphim, her will being fully conformed to the Divine Will. In her beautiful soul all is light, beauty and harmony. Her body is most pure, immaculate; her purity is angelic. She is most faithful, and abandons herself entirely to God; her intention is always pure and most perfect, her love of God most fervent. It was her strong, continual, and interior love that made her surpass not only the love of all the Saints, but even that of all the Seraphim. Her humility was most profound, she always sought seclusion, and kept secret from everyone, and even from herself, her highest gifts. Her charity for her neighbour was like a sweet balsam; all the miseries of the world seemed to find a place in her heart so sweet and merciful by its very nature.

∽

And to-day, oh, daughters, what are we to say of the characteristics of Mary? Her innate inclination is to diffuse everywhere her graces, to console all, to lead all to the knowledge and love of Jesus Christ. Oh, how beautiful and majestic does Mary appear! She is truly the holy and mystical city of God whose glorious foundations are on the peaks of the most sublime mountains.

∽

But I should never finish talking of Mary, because everywhere we behold her beauty, her power and her majesty. Of her the sea speaks by its immense extent. The waters, with their blue and transparent colours which, like crystals, reflect the colours of the most precious, rare and resplendent stones, are in their mute language like an open book recording the virtues of Mary. I should be happy if I could raise your hearts and souls towards Mary, and infuse in you a strong hope, a firm trust and a true devotion to that sweet and most loving Mother.

∽

When your weaknesses tempt you, run to Mary, invoke Mary, look at this beautiful Morning Star, who by means of her splendour disperses all darkness. If you are in danger, if your hearts are confused, turn to Mary; she is our comfort, our help; turn towards her, and you will be saved. Follow her, and you will not mistake the road that leads to Heaven, for Mary is the Gate of Heaven, and you know it well, for you never tire of singing every evening, "Felix coeli porta." Blessed are you, who follow with fidelity this beautiful devotion of singing every evening in praise of Mary, the Ave Maris Stella.

Week 33

Mary, the New Eve

See how grateful we should be to Christianity, which has raised the dignity of woman, re-establishing her rights, unknown to the pagan nations. Until Mary Immaculate, the Woman by excellence, foretold by the prophets, sighed for by the patriarchs, desired by the people. Dawn of the Sun of Justice, had appeared on earth—what was woman?

∞

But Mary appeared, this new Eve, true Mother of the Living, elected by God to be the Co-Redemptrix of the human race, and a new era arose for woman. She is no longer a slave, but equal to man; no longer a servant, but mistress within her domestic walls; no longer the object of disdain and contempt, but raised to the dignity of Mother and Educator, on whose knee generations are built up.

∞

All this we owe to Mary, and in the midst of the tenderness that naturally arises in our hearts for such a pious, amiable, good and condescending Mother, ever ready to listen to our prayers, ever ready to come to our aid, we must not forget what Christian society owes to her, and, consequently, what our obligations are to her.

∞

Mary derives all her greatness from Jesus. If it was her boast that she became the Mother of the Redeemer, to her also, as the Holy Father has said, was consigned the office of guarding and preparing the Victim of the human race. Mary was the Mother of Jesus, not only in the joy of Bethlehem, but also on Calvary, where she not only contemplated the cruel spectacle, but rejoiced at seeing her Son offered for the redemption of mankind. Thus did she most worthily merit to become the Co-Redemptrix.

If, then, we wish to reach the height of the importance of our Mission, let us banish all vanity and levity, and remember that we shall only be true women, when, by the discharge of the principal duties that are imposed upon us, we become the true educators of society, Angels of the family and faithful imitators of Mary Immaculate. But what have you to do to imitate her? I should love you to look upon your Morning Star, Mary, and become so many copies of Mary Immaculate.

Cast an interior glance on your Mother, and, if your eyes cannot sustain the vivid light that radiates from Her, listen to what St. Anselm says of her: "Mary was docile, spoke little; she was always composed, was never heard laughing aloud, nor ruffled or disturbed; she persevered in the reading of the Sacred Scriptures, in mortification and in the works of mercy."

My Thoughts and Prayers

Week 34

Mary, the Immaculate Dove

Holy Church in her earliest days appeared to be all concentrated in Mary, all hearts turned to her, all hopes after Jesus were placed in her. She was the Ark animated by God that contained the Law of the New Alliance, the living Rule of the precepts and counsels of Jesus Christ, the treasure of the wisdom and knowledge of God.

Saint Ambrose says: "Her movement was not indolent, her walk not too quick, her voice not affected or sharp; the composure of her person showed the beauty and harmony of her interior. It was a wonderful spectacle to see with what promptness and diligence she performed her domestic duties, to which she applied herself with great solicitude, but always with tranquility and great peace. Her forehead was serene, and a modesty more celestial than terrestrial pervaded her every movement. Her words were few and always dignified, prudent and joyful. In Mary, all and everything was well regulated."

The difficulties of the primitive Church are just the same after twenty centuries, and it is not to be wondered at, for Christ has always been the sign of contradiction. And so it must be with His Spouse, the Church, in this vale of misery and tears. Do not fear difficulties. Let us raise our eyes to our Heavenly Star.

Let us call upon Mary. She is to us what she was to the Apostles and first Christians. Let us honor this Immaculate Dove, and let us trust her with unlimited trust. The eyes of her soul and mind are turned towards us. Her eyes are sharper and more penetrating than those of the prophets and seers of Judah, more perfect than those of the Ecstatic of Patmos, higher than the angelic hierarchies.

How admirable is Mary Immaculate! Let us abandon ourselves into her hands. She is, I repeat, our august Queen and Mother. Under her mantle we shall be safe.

Dressed in rose gown and shining blue mantle, Mary tenderly opens wide her arms to gather her devoted daughter to her breast. That fortunate soul remarked that she never saw a picture, no matter how beautiful, that could resemble the loving and beautiful virgin of this vision.

My Thoughts and Prayers

Week 35

The Sacred Heart

Behold that Divine Heart! He is our comfort, our way and our life. Listen to Him with great faith and devotion. He will tell you all that I desire from you. He will tell you how I love to have you pure, immaculate, very humble, charitable, fervent, detached from all the follies of this world, and, above all, from your own judgment and self-love. He will tell you also how I desire you all to be full of zeal and fervour for the conversion of souls.

Let us seek the right and sure path of perfection, encouraging ourselves in true Charity towards God and towards our neighbour. The one should never be separated from the other. We should endeavour to attract to the Sacred Heart all those who approach us; that is the object of the life of the Missionary, the Spouse of Jesus Christ.

Blessed Margaret Mary Alacoque saw beautifully engraved in the most Sacred Heart of Jesus the names of those who sought to make It known, and the Divine Heart made known to her that these should never be blotted out. The fire of His love is great and wants to spread, and those souls who endeavour to extend It are loved in a very special manner and filled with celestial graces. Which one of us would not like to be that soul? Otherwise we should be like the foolish Virgins, who, for want of reflection, became unworthy of seeing their

Spouse and entering with Him into the marriage feast.
Let us always have our lamps burning, never weary, and,
as soon as we see our oil is diminishing, let us go to
the Fountain of Life with profound humility to renew
ourselves and to gain new courage.

Little time remains, so let us hurry and work, for the
reward is already prepared, and will be in the measure
that we have prepared it. Jesus is with us. We can do
all things with Him. By ourselves we fall, but with God
all things are possible.

My Thoughts and Prayers

Missionaries of the Sacred Heart

Love ought to transform us all. But what are the necessary means for obtaining this transformation? The first is to approach the Sacred Heart of Jesus in a spirit of humility and confidence; the second is to let grace work in us, following its impulses with fidelity and constancy.

⁓

The good Jesus, through the goodness of His Divine Heart, makes known to us our ugliness and our misery; but we should not fly away frightened by the knowledge we receive of ourselves, we should rather humble ourselves and beg God to free us from our misery. Be not discouraged at seeing yourselves so far from the perfection of Holy Love, because Jesus desires to grant it to you, to help you in your own efforts. It suffices if we have recourse to Him with a sincere desire to correspond with His graces and to trust entirely to His Love.

⁓

Let us throw ourselves into the blessed flames of the most Sacred Heart of Jesus, and let that holy fire burn into our spirit, so that it may destroy, purify, renew and sanctify all our thoughts, affections, sentiments, intentions and desires. What have we to fear if the most Sacred Heart protects us?

⁓

And what may we not hope for, if we confide in the Heart of such a compassionate and powerful Father? Let us fix our gaze on the Wound of the Sacred Heart of Jesus. We shall read in characters of blood the height and depth of the love that He bears us, and we shall always feel, wherever we are, comforted in hoping for everything from His infinite goodness.

∞

Very often our prayers are imperfect and deserve to be rejected by God; but the loving Heart of Jesus sanctifies them. He Himself asks for us that which He sees will be for our greater good, and compassionately covers our unworthiness with His merits.

∞

Through your goodness, you made me a Missionary of your Sacred Heart; therefore I am also to make reparation. My Jesus, you already know my fervent desires; move the hearts of my helpers and grant success soon to those works.

My Thoughts and Prayers

Week 37

The Divine Heart

In the secrecy of the Holy Tabernacle the loving Heart of Jesus takes note of our needs in order to help us, and waits for nothing more than to see us at His feet, full of confidence, uniting our prayers with His.

Recall often what Jesus said to Saint Gertrude, His Beloved, "Here is My Heart, avail yourself of It to make good what is deficient in your prayers." Another time, Saint Gertrude, full of love, made a fervent prayer (and this is especially good for the Missionary) in which she declared that if it were necessary to travel the whole world barefooted till the Day of Judgment, in order to lead all men to the Heart of Jesus, she would have done so with her whole heart, and would have carried every one of them in her arms so as to satisfy, at least in part, the infinite desires of His sweet Divine Love. Even more, if it were possible, she would divide her heart into as many parts as were necessary to give a portion to all men on earth, and thus infuse into them the good desire to serve God, and thus give perfect joy to His Divine Heart. Then Jesus appeared to her showing her the gift He was about to give her, in the form of a very rich treasure sent by the Holy Trinity, and whilst this gift appeared to rise in the heavens, the Angels seemed to prostrate themselves before Him. She knew, then, that when prayers and holy desires are offered to God, the whole celestial court receives and raises them to His throne, as gifts most pleasing to God, and that when to one's merits the merits of Jesus Christ are joined, the very Saints themselves respect them.

~

Let us fly, fly, dear children, often to the Tabernacle — as the hart panteth after the fountains of clear water. As long as we live in this exile, far from the heavenly country, let us not rest, but labour until we repose in the Heart of Him Whom we love so ardently, as true Spouses and Missionaries of the Sacred Heart. Let us always go to His Divine Heart, think of Him, fly to Him, sigh for Him alone and always, because the vehemence of His love for us, is truly wonderful.

My Thoughts and Prayers

Week 38

The Blessed Sacrament

By the words of consecration said by the priest in the name of Jesus, the bread is changed or transubstantiated into the body of Jesus, and so the body and blood are present under the appearances of bread and of wine by a miracle of the Omnipotent. After the Consecration, the substance of the bread and wine disappear, the appearances only remaining, like so many veils of love and wisdom to hide from our material eyes our glorious Lord's presence, as also to supply motives for faith, confidence and courage in receiving our Divine Lord into our hearts.

As long as the species remains, so long does the Sacramental Presence last; as soon as the species is consumed, the most Sacred Body retires and vanishes. Nothing but wonders are worked on the Altar. The priests, who, during the twenty-four hours, offer the Divine Sacrifice in so many countries, towns and villages all the world over, are innumerable, and thus in a hundred thousand places Jesus is present in the Sacrament of His Love. Could there be an invention more beautiful and more holy than the Institution of this Most Divine Sacrament? Could the Loving Jesus show us a greater tenderness of love? But remember, daughters, that this most Holy Sacrament is like the column of fire that lighted and guided the Israelites to the Promised Land, yet proved dark for the Egyptians. This mystery of the Holy Eucharist is like that of the Cross, a scandal to the impious and the wise of this world, but to humble believers a source of virtue and of the wisdom of God.

∞

Our Savior hides his divine perfections from our eyes in the Blessed Sacrament. He does this not to deceive us, but to make our hearts feel the depth of his immense humility, so that we would pledge ourselves to imitate him.

∞

Let us pray to the Sacred Heart of Jesus, asking him to change the coldness of our hearts toward him into an ardent desire to love, please and possess him.

∞

Frequent spiritual communions will animate your confidence in the Sacred Heart of Jesus, who is the God of your heart and your inheritance forever. The ardent desire to have Jesus Christ come into our hearts to take possession and reign there as God, must persuade us to give all to him without reserve, to dispose our souls to receive him in the best way possible.

∞

In the Holy Eucharist Jesus becomes all to all. For each one he makes himself little and satisfies all: from the vast and profound genius that longs to know him, to the simple and naive intelligence, barely developed who only asks for that learning that is necessary to believe and to love. The science of the saints consists in knowing God and in knowing oneself; in knowing what is the end of our life and what are the means of arriving at it. The practice of this science is summed up in these words: love of God and neighbor, true humility and accomplishment of the obligations of our state.

Week 39

Humility

Last night the weather threatened to break and the Sisters asked me if we were going to have good weather, because if it were bad they had made up their minds where to go and how to spend their time. I told them that if we humbled ourselves profoundly for our faults, holding ourselves to blame for all the acts of frailty that sea-sickness caused us to commit, God would be propitious to us. At first some refused to acknowledge that they were in fault, saying it was the sea that caused so much discomfort, but remembering the promise they had made of suffering willingly for the holy cause of the Mission, they felt themselves obliged to humble themselves profoundly, and our dear Jesus in the truly paternal goodness of His Heart granted us good weather, and so we are all assembled on the first-class deck. You see, humility works wonders. . . .

∞

Let us learn, dear daughters, to become humble, because God loves the humble, whilst He resists the proud. If we elevate ourselves through pride, God will withdraw from us, with the result that we fall into dense darkness. If we are humble, He will approach us, console us and hear our prayer, and He will send us away justified.

∞

No, daughters, God does not make the humble wait long. He runs, flies to satisfy their holy and most excellent desires. It often happens that, drawn by a humble soul, He gives what He has not been asked for. Be humble, daughters dear, the Sacred Heart has prepared many graces in the abundance of His treasures for the Institute. Be humble, His graces are hanging on a thread only. If we are truly humble and simple, these graces will be showered upon us. If we are proud, full of ourselves, He will withdraw His graces. In vain shall we then ask—for He withdraws Himself from the proud and haughty.

⌒∽

Oh, humility, how powerful and beautiful thou art! Do, my daughters, be humble of intellect and thought, as true Religious placed in the school of perfection should be. Have an abject opinion of yourselves. Let each one consider herself the least of all the Sisters and she the only one unworthy to live with the Spouses of Christ, the Beloved of His Most Sacred Heart.

⌒∽

Be grateful of God's mercies, for gratitude is the noble sentiment of humble souls. Be humble, therefore, and always truly so, loving to be held of no account, unnoticed, forgotten, ill-treated, despised and calumniated; even in such cases one should remain calm, resigned and contented, as in a garden of flowers. Prefer to obey rather than to command. When you are corrected, do not justify yourselves, never say, "I speak because I have reason to do so." Keep silent and practise virtue whether you are right or wrong, otherwise we may dream of perfection, but we shall never reach it.

◦

With humility, you will increase in grace and virtue, the serenity of the Angels will shine upon your faces, you will not be discouraged in adversity nor elated in prosperity. Your only thought will be to please Jesus in everything, and then you will be like those pure white doves, beautiful and lovely in the sight of God. Your voice will be sweet to the Sacred Heart of Jesus, your prayer will be as perfume in the sight of the Most High, your life will be as a burning lamp in the Community; in fine, your death will be that of the Just, with an immense trust in Him Whom you have imitated, and Who is your All and the Centre of your aspirations.

◦

Humility is the foundation of faith. Since faith, the beautiful daughter of God, is the cornerstone of our religion, the basis of Christian discipline and the beginning of eternal life, it is evident that the price and the excellence of humility are beyond compare (Matt. 8:8).

Week 40

Humility, the
Foundation of Virtue

Humility is the secret that penetrates the walls of the Holy City and the rock of the Omnipotent. Humility is the foundation of every meritorious and virtuous work and of prayer. It is impossible to please God without humility; it is a golden scale that measures the strength of our prayers, and it is, therefore, the measure of their weight in God's own scales.

∞

The humblest obtain the most graces, the least humble obtain the least grace, for it is written: God resists the proud and gives grace to the humble. "Deus superbis resistit; humilibus autem dat gratiam." Chase away all sentiments of pride and self-love if you want God to be with you. God will be our strength, and if we are humble our prayers will ascend, like a sweet perfume, to the throne of Heaven, where they will be fully granted. The humble Religious is like a bunch of Spikenard, which, though the smallest and humblest of flowers, is one of the most fragrant. Spread about you the perfume of humility, study profoundly this celestial virtue until you possess it completely and perfectly, and then you will be able to repeat some day, when this life is over, with the Spouse of the Canticles, "Nardus mea dedit odorem suavitatis," while the loving Saviour, delighting in your sweet virtue, will give you the eternal kiss of Peace.

∞

It is in Retreat that we learn to humble ourselves and to earn the precious gem of humility. If we become careless and ignorant in our spiritual life, we think ourselves better than we are. But, in solitude we are enabled to understand well what the Beloved Disciple meant when he admonishes us and says, "If we say we have no faults, we deceive ourselves, and the truth is not in us." Our misery is indeed great. Ignorance, blindness of intellect, pride of mind and heart, inclination to vice, repugnance to virtue, readiness for evil, and sloth in doing good—all of these are a sufficient motive for humbling ourselves in the most pure presence of God, and confessing that we are truly dust and ashes: nothing in fine.

Let us weigh carefully, dear children, what a great misfortune it is not to have humility, for the lack of this precious pearl places a wall of bronze between us and God. If we are not humble, we shall derive no advantage from the ways that lead to humility, for whatever may be our fault against humility, though it appears small, it does us a great injury, for faults against humility are severely punished by God.

Be, therefore, watchful, children, and guard that precious and holy humility, for none of the lovely works of piety prescribed by the Holy Institute can be carried out without humility, and your many and good prayers will not be helpful to you without a humble heart. We must pray much to obtain this great and precious gift of humility, for we must be humble if we want to be heard. Mary, our tender Mother, teaches us this by her example, because if God loved her for her virginity, He loved her more on account of her humility, as Saint Bernard affirms.

Many often complain of not being heard, though they pray much, but, if they become humble, as Jesus desires, and practise humility, then they will be heard quickly, for the key which opens the celestial treasures is humility. Let us please God, children, and give glory to Him. Let us console the Adorable Heart of Jesus by becoming truly humble. Let us practise always and in every event great simplicity and humility, which is the glorious chain which unites us with God. No, you cannot stand without Jesus; He is for you a blessed necessity. The soul yearns for its Creator, its Centre, its Beginning, its Beloved. Remove, then, any impediment produced by the want of humility, and then nothing will hinder you. Your wings will be free, and you will fly with all the vehemence and ardour of which the soul is capable unto your Treasure, Who will allow you to taste an anticipated Heaven which is the sure noviciate [sic] of eternal life. The peace and joy which God infuses into the humble soul exceed all understanding.

Week 41

Obedience

Oh, obedience, how dear to the Heart of Jesus! Obedient souls delight His Heart Divine. They are His Kingdom, His heaven, His glory. To them He communicates His lights, His gifts, His graces, and often He admits them to His secrets. On them He sheds the rays of His countenance, and renders them perfectly happy in their state. Through obedience, Jesus accomplishes His greatest designs and works on this earth. To our dear Lord, these acts of His Spouses are more gratifying than a thousand sacrifices made from caprice and one's own will. Jesus loves to stay with obedient Religious. He guides them with His wisdom, fills them with His treasures and comforts them with His abundant graces.

Oh, happy obedience! Do love this virtue, dear daughters, let it be your favourite. If you are obedient, you will be true Missionaries, you will be blessed abundantly by Jesus and you will save a great number of souls who await your work.

None of you should work from self-will. You should have no thought contrary to obedience, but submit as so many little lambs. This is the secret of obtaining peace, and of obtaining great graces and blessings for the Institute. Love virtue, but obedience and humility above all, because with obedience you have given what is yours to God. Be obedient and your sacrifice will be entire, you will be true Spouses of Christ, you will enjoy Heaven in anticipation.

❧

Do not have any will of your own, and then you will not make your Superiors suffer. Why should you suffer for the devil? Why should you make a purgatory for yourselves and make others suffer? Why lose peace and make everything desolate on account of your own fancies and caprices? Submit yourself to the sweet yoke of obedience and you will become a haven of Christ, a haven of peace for all your Sisters.

❧

In martyrdom we sacrifice the body, in obedience we sacrifice the will, our liberty, the supreme power of the soul. Obedience is a penance of the mind, a sacrifice immensely more pleasing to God than any other sacrifice you could voluntarily make of your own choice. One act of obedience is more pleasing to God than a thousand other acts of your own will. The Saints teach us that it is better to eat by virtue of obedience than to fast to gratify one's own will.

❧

Saint Mary Magdalen de Pazzi, used to say that the simplest act of obedience is greater than the highest act of contemplation. In fact, we read in her life that when she was in ecstasy the voice of obedience was sufficient to recall her to herself. Learn to love this virtue, which forms the character of a true Religious.

To share the love of the Heart of Jesus means to share with Christ the obedience of the Cross which makes reparation for disobedience and alleviates the moral and physical suffering which are the result.

Week 42

Happiness and
Faithfulness

Every time we come on deck we look for a place to be alone, but after a few minutes we are surrounded by the ladies of the first-class deck, who follow us with their chairs. They appear to be nice people, and to like the Catholic Religion. The Captain and other passengers are most anxious to make us comfortable. All delight in seeing us happy and free from sickness. After all, happiness follows us everywhere.

⌒〇

Oh, would that God were really appeased; let us no longer offend Him. Do not arouse His wrath by infidelity to grace. Let us trust in the help of our good God, for of ourselves we can do nothing, not even can we pronounce with merit His adorable name. Let us endeavour to be faithful to His holy help, through the merits of Jesus Christ and with the help of His sweet powerful Mother.

⌒〇

Our faith obliges us to trust in God, and that trust will make us strong even unto death.

⌒〇

Be faithful to what you have undertaken, try to understand the prodigies of love which God has worked in you, learn the language of the Saints, who, on gazing at the heavens, earth and sea, and the starry firmament, repeated within themselves that holy refrain, "Love God and serve Him with fidelity."

∽

The Holy Prophet David mentions very often in his psalms the kindness of God, awakening in his own heart deep sentiments of gratitude; he, whose heart was made like unto the beautiful heart of God. Yes, every grace which you have received is a special token of God's love for you; the multiplicity and frequency of graces does not diminish, but, rather, increases the value and renders it more valuable.

∽

Blessed will you be, my daughters, if, knowing the gifts of God, you render yourselves more worthy to receive greater gifts.

My Thoughts and Prayers

Week 43

Faith and Trust

Remember, daughters, that our trust in Jesus is our very life, and we must always hope in Him and in the goodness of His Most Adorable Heart against every hope. It may at times appear that He overlooks the evil that we suffer; but, no. He is awake. He watches over us and all our interests. It is He who brings forth the lilies of the valley and the flowers of the fields, but He thinks more of us, as we are the elect portion of His Divine Heart....

We are dedicated to Him as Missionaries of His Divine Heart. Yes, my daughters, as long as you have the grace to combat faithfully under the standard of the Missionaries of the Sacred Heart, you will always walk under the protection of a special Providence. But an exact fidelity is necessary to merit such a protection. You are certainly resolved to be thus faithful, but you must also supplicate the good Jesus to place His seal upon your arm so that you may never need to lean on human creatures and to put a seal on your heart, so that you will love Him only and will work for Him alone.

Ask Him to seal with His Holy Name all your thoughts, words and actions, all your sufferings, your joys and aspirations. Beg Him to live always in you and you in Him, so that you may always be one with Him, that you may always glorify Him, and not bear in vain the noble and enviable title of Missionaries of His Divine Heart.

❦

Let us have confidence, dear daughters, unlimited confidence, and, like brave champions, we shall weaken the strength of the enemy and conquer him, and make everything redound to the glory of God and the consolation of His Divine Heart.

❦

Thanksgiving is a perfect act of love, because in it we have no other interest than the glory of God, the pleasure of God, the complacency of God. When we ask, we are moved by our own interest, but when we thank, we are moved by more noble and more perfect sentiments. Let us repeat, children, let us repeat the hymn of thanksgiving which, like a blessed and ardent arrow coming from our hearts, will fly to and wound the Heart of our most loving Spouse and Benefactor.

❦

The flame of the love of God will not die in you, for it is like fire. The more it spreads and increases, the more it requires to be fed. Love is the fountain of grace, and grace has a sublime power of attraction. Love is industrious, and becomes, by way of superhuman effort, like unto the most pure gold of perfection. It conquers sorrows, persecutions and difficulties. May the good Jesus love us accordingly and accompany us always with every grace. Often you complain of being far away from Jesus. That is not so—He follows you everywhere.

Be faithful. Leave the common ways. Walk swiftly in His footsteps, and, sanctifying yourselves, you will save many souls who will follow your example and listen to your words. If you love God with great fidelity, it will follow that all your actions, sufferings and affections will be marked with the Divine Seal, so that your fidelity, your loving work, which, in its beginnings is like a small stream, will grow in its admirable course and became like a broad river.

Week 44

Serenity

We, leaning on our Beloved Jesus, have always remained serene even in the stormiest weather. Some priests on board would say often to us, "But you are always happy, like those who have a clear conscience." I do not know if we really have a clear conscience, but I do know we trust the Most Sacred Heart of Our Lord Jesus, and, leaning on Him, we do not fear, knowing well that He has a special care of us, and that not one hair of our heads shall be touched without His permission.

Oh, yes, the Missionary of the Sacred Heart bears the seal of God, and proves to all that her election to such a state comes not from nature but from grace. His Divine Will, the extension of the Kingdom of Jesus Christ, is all that concerns us, so that the luminous and glorious motto of the Missionary of the Sacred Heart is always and everywhere—"All to the greater glory of the Most Sacred Heart of Jesus," and in difficulties, "Omnia possum in Eo qui me confortat."

Always appreciate the great gift God has given you by calling you to Holy Religion. He alone, the Master elects, calls and destines His Creatures to the noble state, the high dignity of becoming His Spouses. Yes! God alone, through His Divine goodness, chooses for His glory a weak, fragile creature. No, it is not nature that can claim supernatural graces and gifts of grace, but the goodness and benignity of God, who raises nature to a celestial life. It is not nature that renders herself superior to her strength, but Divine Grace which condescends to human weakness and thus manifests the absolute authority of God over us, while it discloses again His infinite mercy and goodness by raising us poor human creatures to the Divine nuptials. Dear children! it is only by an ineffable condescension that God deigns to strengthen our fragile clay, to sanctify it, to purify it, and to render it capable of becoming a precious instrument in the Religious House, in the Church, both Militant and Triumphant.

At the end of the Retreat you will have the good fortune of renewing your vows. This renewal is a new promise of a sincere and generous offering which we make to our Divine Spouse, and it is a real glory to be dedicated and consecrated to Him. To renew our vows is to renew our Profession, to offer to the Lord the new fruits of the same tree, and to burn on the same Altar of our heart new grains of incense, in the odour of sweetness, to the Divine Heart.

My Thoughts and Prayers

Week 45

Conquering Human Respect

Remember, however, dear daughters, that it is not enough to live in a holy land to be holy; rather, it is necessary to live saintly, according to the Rules, and in the actual exercise of virtue. One cannot be called holy who merely belongs to a family of Saints, if he does not walk in the footsteps of the Saints. Our Divine Master, our most loving Spouse Himself, tells us so, "Not those who say Lord, Lord, shall enter Heaven, but those who do the Will of My Father."

❧

"My heart is ready, O God, my heart is ready." (Ps. 108:1). Yes, my heart is ready, my God, speak; ask of me whatever you please; I will accept any sacrifice in order to grow in your love and to promote your glory. Heart of Jesus, I abandon myself to you. Speak to me, instruct me, illuminate me! (Ps. 25:5).

❧

To lose confidence in God is an insult to him because it is telling him that he has failed us, which is impossible, whereas it is always we who fail by placing impediments to the operation of grace. Therefore, in the future, instead of failing to trust him, I will humbly trust him, knowing that the more I acknowledge my weakness, the greater opportunity the Almighty has to show his goodness.

❧

It is really sad that so many follow the devil and not Christ. We are so cowardly, that, whether it be from human respect or some other motive, we fear to speak of Christ in public. We see virtue derided, and we remain silent. Why are we so cowardly? We should strengthen our faith in an endeavour to imbue others with the spirit of Christ and to become animated ourselves with the true charity of the Divine Heart, and thus proclaim the truth. Do not be afraid of offending those who approach us, or of being importunate when speaking the truths of our faith. No, if we are filled with the sweet kind charity of Christ, coupled with strength and energy, no one will take offence but rather be conquered.

Yes, if there is true charity, the most Sacred Heart will be honoured. Sometimes a person will not speak deliberately of our Holy Religion, but praises vice rather than virtue, because such an one has lost his bearings, but if it were possible to find one individual who, with the generous charity and the sweetness of the Sacred Heart of Jesus, could introduce the subject of our Faith gently, correct certain wrong ideas, little by little such a good person would conquer that soul and reunite it with that secure trunk of truth from which unconsciously it has become detached. If such a spirit is necessary everywhere, what must be the necessity of it for those nations who once were profoundly religious, and now, through pride, ambition and a false sense of freedom, have allowed themselves to be carried away and to do what they do not want to do. People on board are already saying, "Why are these Missionaries going to America, while in Europe there are worse despisers of religion and faith?" These words went to my very heart. If I were not wounded by such expressions, I should not be a true daughter of the Church nor would I have any love for my country. Such expressions dishonor nations, which in olden times flourished amidst true and profoundly religious sentiments.

Week 46

Conquering Sin

"But I am weak!" With God's help we can do everything; He never fails a humble and faithful soul. "But I am so fragile!" If you are humble and constant, God will be your strength, and, having been made strong with the strength of God, what shall we fear? The devil is terrible, but he is like a chained dog—he cannot disturb you or hurt you without God's permission. Therefore, a humble and faithful soul need have no fear of the devil. "I have failed in generosity, I have fallen at the first temptation, now I shall not be able to do anything well." Have you fallen? Then, humble yourself, and, with a lively act of contrition from the depths of your heart, ask pardon with great humility and renew your promises to God and those who represent Him; then be up and doing with more courage than ever to repair your defects.

∞

In order not to fall into sin we need to continually distrust ourselves and the virtues which self-love make us believe we have acquired and trust wholeheartedly in the help of God.

∞

The faults of which we have repented will appear covered with jewels on the last day.

∞

Without the practice of our spiritual duties, it is impossible to remain free of defects.

∽

Let us also be faithful to the operations of the Holy Spirit in our souls! Let our minds be pure, disinterested, humble, pliant, and then we shall see what beautiful and wonderful things the Holy Ghost will work in our souls. Even the Angelic Spirits would fall into an ecstasy of wonder at the marvelous workings of the Holy Spirit. It is a work worthy of the Infinite Wisdom and Goodness of God. This Spirit works within us, inspires us, instructs us, encourages us, and comforts us with His abundant and perennial lights, with His promptings and impulses in every holy work. Finally, He surrounds us with loving solicitude in keeping us within the enclosure of His eternal and infinite love.

My Thoughts and Prayers

Week 47

The Church Militant
and Church Suffering

How fruitful is the blessing of the Holy Father! I would wish everyone to understand this, and put confidence in the Pope. Who is the Holy Father? He is the representative of God, of His authority and His majesty amongst men. The Holy Father is the instrument of the Holy Spirit; the depository of the treasures and secrets of God. He is the Key of Knowledge for the Christian People! he has in his keeping the power to loose and bind sin. The voice of the Holy Father is the voice of God; his word is the word of God. He is the living ark of the new alliance in which is found the Divine Law, the Manna of Celestial Doctrine, the precious vase of gold, in which is contained the purity of the Catholic Faith. The Pope is the guide of the people, the ark of salvation for all. He, in the name of Jesus Christ, has the virtue to raise and save Society from its sickness and oppression, if only it will allow itself to be cured and healed by him.

∞

The Pope is the shining lighthouse of Divine Wisdom, and so his words and his blessings are that true column of fire that guides me in every danger and every difficulty. Do pray, daughters, pray for the Holy Father, pray for the Ruler of Church's destiny, pray for him in these difficult times. We must do so, as we are under obligations of filial gratitude to Leo XIII, who loves and favours our beloved Institute as if it were his own beloved family. Speak, children, to everybody concerning the Pope. Make them unite themselves with him, for he who is united closely with the Pope, however far he may have strayed from the right path, returns to God's ways in the end.

~

These Blessed Souls cannot help themselves, but they can do so much for us. Let us have pity on them; let them have the principal part of our prayers, for the mitigation of their sufferings depends upon our charity and our prayers. One might almost say the keys of their prison have been consigned to us. The Holy Souls love their Divine Spouse, they desire Him, they sigh for Him, but they need the cooling hand of benefactors to cancel their debts. These doves would love to fly to the bosom of their God, but, woe to them if no pitying hand severs their chains of fire. Come, beloved daughters, draw down upon them a celestial dew which will cool and allay their inconceivable heat. Your prayers will be the dew that will quench the flames of Divine Justice. Comply with the just desires of these souls. You will be doing much to your own advantage if you relieve them by offering for them your Holy Communions, Indulgences, Masses and all satisfactory works. This, you see, will be a work of perfect charity, of immense glory to God, of great joy to the Church Militant, Suffering and Triumphant, because with your prayers you will send many saintly souls to the Kingdom of the Blessed.

~

Have no fear that you will lose your prayers, indulgences and satisfactory works by giving them to the Holy Souls, but, rather, rest assured that by so doing you will become rich in grace and merits in this life and in sublime glory in Paradise. Rest satisfied also that the intrinsic merit of this work of suffrage remains always with you, being of its nature inalienable; only the portion that gives atonement goes to the Holy Souls. Giving up, then, this portion of our works to the Holy Souls, which some do by means of the Heroic Act, we do nothing less than convert every act of satisfaction into merit, and be assured that in the scales of God one degree of grace and merit is of more value than all the works of atonement we may apply to the Holy Souls.

⁓

Be generous to the Holy Souls, for he who gives shall receive, and he who is merciful shall obtain mercy. The souls whom we set free will become so many advocates, so many protectors who will pray for us, intercede for us, and, what is more, they will interest themselves in our Eternal Salvation.

Week 48

The Power of Prayer

What a gift prayer is! It is the real treasure of our soul, our being able to give to God the worship of perfect adoration. Prayer is the channel through which the most precious waters of grace continually and copiously flow from the Heart of God.

∞

Prayer is powerful! It fills the earth with mercy, it makes the Divine clemency pass from generation to generation; right along the course of the centuries wonderful works have been achieved through prayer. We are the dust of the earth, and our days are like the grass. Man is here on a pilgrimage, and shortly will be no more, but the mercy and clemency obtained through the power of prayer will always produce in people generous and salutary effects.

∞

Love us, Jesus, with Your sweet chains.
Of that pure love we fain would claim;
Our wings to Heaven we open wide.
To leave low earth, and there abide.

∞

"I will lead my beloved into the solitude, and there I will speak to her, heart to heart." Jesus Christ Himself frequently retired alone into the mountains and into the quiet Garden of Olives to converse with His Eternal

Father in the silence of the night. In retirement and solitude we are disposed to speak with God confidentially and to beg Him to fill us with His grace. It is in Retreat that we learn the multiform and precious ways of prayer. It is there we learn to pray, whether it be by means of the tongue, good works, or sufferings. It is there one acquires the spirit of interior prayer so sublime and rich with merits, for it is the interior spirit that raises us up at every moment and in every work to God. It is in Retreat that the soul learns to give internal glances at the beauty and goodness of God. These glances are like a melodious prayer, pleasing to the Divine Heart of the loving Jesus.

God is a most pure Spirit, and He loves, with a special love and very dearly, pure and immaculate hearts, and their loving, simple looks please Him. When can we better simplify and purify our spirit than during Retreat? The soul learns to love God as He should be loved, so worthy of all our love. Then, also, these internal aspirations, however short, leave incredible power within, and are very profitable to us and give great glory to God. The soul learns that there is no necessity to look for her beloved outside her own being, and that she can find Him within herself, as on His own throne and in His tabernacle. The soul drinks in large draughts from that wonderful spring, the Wound of the Sacred Heart of Jesus.

It is in Retreat that the Missionary learn[s] what is required in order to become rich for eternity, and acquires at the same time a loving and continual purity of intention. Oh, how precious it is! The most vigilant in this exercise of the inner life have the richest graces in this life and the greatest glory in the next. Yes, my children, God is the beginning, the centre and the end of all our daily actions, and whilst as Missionaries of His Divine Heart we give great and continual glory to God, we also acquire for ourselves at every moment immense treasures of grace. Whether we work, eat, teach or sleep, or voyage, let us do all in the name of Jesus and in that of His Divine Heart.

Now, here is the second thing I would ask of you. Be calm and composed. Place all your trust in God. This is not presumption, as you have worked and studied hard all the year, so don't alarm yourselves. Study quietly. Pray, and confide in your Mother, Mary Immaculate, and all will go well. He who trusts in Her shall not be confounded.

Week 49

Charity

Those souls united in Charity peacefully repose in God, and await with security great graces from God's goodness. Magnanimous and generous souls are those united in Charity; they are blessed by God; they soar on high; they ascend to Heaven, where they repose at God's feet, and He, rejoicing in them, crowns them with glory.

∞

What a wonderful sight to see so many souls of different nations and different languages united in one religious family, joined by the ties of the sweet Charity of the Adorable Heart of Jesus.

∞

Though Charity signifies that form of union which necessarily unites all members of Religious Orders, nevertheless there is another union which each one should possess within herself. Our Divine Lord said that prayer is heard when two are united in His name — for example, when the exterior man and interior man are united; the soul and the body; the subjection of the body to the spirit; these two must join together.

∞

So, to pray we must unite the body with its feelings to the soul with its imaginations and desires, with its superior powers, memory, understanding and will. Christ then shall be in your midst, united in His name, helping you to pray with efficacy. He cannot pray whose soul is in disorder, whose mind is wandering with a thousand useless, vain and anxious thoughts. The Spirit of God shuns, such a soul, and so the poor soul, deprived of help from on high, languishes little by little and gradually loses the spirit of prayer.

Oh, if I could but open the purses of many of the rich to whom the good God has given so liberally of this earth's treasures! If I could only make them understand what a reward theirs would be, if, prompted by their own good heart, they would come to our aid in succouring these poor creatures who still live in darkness. By so doing they would be placing their generous offerings in the Bank of Heaven, where they would fructify a hundredfold, if not in this world, certainly in the next, and their generosity would make them happy with an eternal felicity in Heaven, where God has prepared a profusion of immense treasures for the merciful.

Whenever, due to my lack of charity, I observe faults in others, I will seek to excuse the intention even when I cannot excuse the action. Never judge if you do not wish to be judged by Jesus Christ.

Jesus, envelop me in your charity so I can truly be a Missionary of your divine heart, never carrying this noble title in vain. I love you, my Jesus, I love you so much, so very much; with your grace, I always want to love you more.

Week 50

The World to Come

May God bless you and close you in His Adorable Heart, wherein resides the throne of peace, an anticipated Heaven. Love Jesus much, and think of nothing else. Work with great zeal for the glory of God, under the banner of holy Obedience.

Do not seek rest on this earth, but be ready to die on the battlefield in company with Jesus, with the assurance that the more you fight the greater will be your crown, a crown that in Eternity no one can usurp.

Now that the voyage is at an end, we feel it parting from these poor people who trusted us so much and for whom we have been able to do some good. Oh! if only we could again impress upon them the happiness that awaits them if they are faithful to prayer and to the Sacraments. If we could make them understand that Heaven is the great prize or reward granted to good Christians, to those who are faithful to the laws of Jesus Christ! Oh, Heaven! Who can conceive or express the inconceivable delights that God has prepared for those who serve Him with that internal and external worship He requires of us?

The Holy Prophet spoke well when he said, "Rejoice and be glad ye who love the Lord." "Drink large draughts of that river of peace." "Fill yourselves with joy, glory and happiness, because the Lord has said: I shall pour upon Jerusalem celestial torrents of glory that will inundate it with the purest consolations and delights." On that most blessed Eternal Day we shall be rapt in ecstasies of love and gratitude, and there will be an immense jubilee contemplating God face to face. We shall be rapt in His infinite beauty, illuminated by His light, inebriated by His peace, fortified by His Divine Consolations, because to see God and to contemplate His Divine Beauty means to love Him with the most pure and most perfect love, and that love will augment in us joy and contentment and the enjoyment of our souls. Speak often of Heaven to those who approach you, make them love it as well as the virtues which are required before we can be admitted to our blessed country. For if you know how to draw souls there by your zeal, your good example and your exemplary religious conduct, you may be assured the Gates will be opened for you also.

My Thoughts and Prayers

Week 51

Eternal Love

My beloved is more beautiful than the sun; he surpasses every beauty that exists. The light is beautiful, but he is more so because he, my treasure, is the splendor of the eternal light. He is the majesty of God. I love my beloved: I love him so much I am consumed with love. Enlarge my heart, beloved of my soul and render me a bit more capable for I cannot withstand your love anymore, ocean of infinite love, I want to love you; but the more I love you, the less I love, because I want to love you all the more. I can't go on anymore—enlarge … spread wide my heart.

The soul perfectly abandoned in the arms of the omnipotent does not desire or relish any more the things of the earth once she rejoices only in God. Whatever the dispositions of providence for her (since she has already surrendered herself), she finds in those designs a transcendent joy and great purity. She discovers that joy beyond compare that flows in torrents from his heart. As much as it is possible in this land of exile, it is like the joy the blessed in heaven taste in following the all-holy God.

We seem to see the portals of Heaven which do not close at the end of the day, because there daytime never ends, for the day up there is eternal and the light which emanates from the Divine Face never fails. There, in

that abode, exists no night, no ignorance, no blindness, for everything is seen in God; there, no sorrows
exist, no tears, no adversity, no sighs. No, daughters, in
Heaven there are no clouds to obscure the Divine Sun,
the Eternal Sun of Justice. There is no fear of losing
God; no wiles of the enemy, for he has been routed;
the world is far away, and the body spiritualized lives in
harmony with the soul. No, there is no night in Heaven
and the door is always open. Friends reach there at
every moment, every instant; they do not disturb, but,
rather, render the repose serene and sweet.

My Thoughts and Prayers

Week 52

The Work Commences: Building the Kingdom of God

I wanted to go to Heaven, but what with one thing and another we have entered the New York Bay. The Superintendent of the Customs House Officers and Doctor are all on board. We are requested to give our names to a New York representative whilst the Fulda is being towed down the bay by three tugs. We disembarked at Hoboken Docks, where we were met by our dear American Sisters, who received us with great joy. A Customs Officer came up, marked our baggage and asked us to say a prayer for him.

I found everything in perfect order here, with much to console me. I cannot, for the present, give you further details, for I have a great number of friends to greet. I will, however, send you further news as soon as I embark on my next voyage.

In the meantime I commend myself to your good prayers, as well as my intentions and new enterprises for the good of souls and the glory of God. I'll work hard and you'll pray, I'm sure, adding some extra sacrifices, especially that of self-abasement. Offer everything as a perfect holocaust to the Adorable Heart of Jesus, Who loves us so much and has done so much to merit for us our beautiful and sublime vocation.

May Jesus bless you and enclose
you in His Sacred Heart.
Your affectionate Mother in Corde Jesu,
Francesca Saverio Cabrini.

My Thoughts and Prayers

Short Quotes

If you desire to convert the whole world, invoke Mary.

The science of suffering is the science of the saints.

Our faith obliges us to trust in God, and that trust will make us strong even unto death.

We had Heaven in our hearts.

The world is too small for what I intend to do.

By ourselves we fall, but with God all things are possible.

Happy the one who, at the tribunal of God, will be able to present herself followed by a great number of souls saved through her.

Afterword

There is a story told by one of St. Frances Xavier Cabrini's biographers that is particularly revealing about her life. Not long after she professed her vows of poverty, chastity, and obedience—vows she had so long desired to make—and was consecrated to the Lord, a small glimpse of her holy virtue was made known. One night, in the old monastery in Italy that Mother Cabrini had turned into an orphanage, the sister who slept in the bed next to her was startled awake to find Mother Cabrini sitting up in bed with a glowing light shining forth from her face. Mother Cabrini appeared transfigured with the beautiful radiance of Christ, her loving Spouse, who had chosen her and called to her throughout her life. Her joyous love for the Lord simply couldn't be contained. This same love shone forth from her for the rest of her life—not as literal light but in the many countless acts of service she humbly performed.

By now, after completing the spiritual journey on which this book has led us, we too have glimpsed the love of Christ that radiated from the life of St. Frances Xavier Cabrini. By her own words and example, she has revealed to us her missionary heart and profound humility in joining her sufferings with Christ's for the redemption of others. She has demonstrated her unwavering faith in Christ, sustained by her devotion to His Sacred Heart, nourished by the Holy Eucharist, and nurtured by our Blessed

Mother, Patroness of Missionaries. And perhaps most importantly, she has radiated the beauty and power of living as a true woman of God. St. Frances Xavier Cabrini built an empire of hope with little more than the habit she wore and the grace of God. She was a mother to her daughters; a teacher, protector, and provider to the orphan girls in her care; a nurturer to the sick; an advocate for those whose voices were not or could not be heard; a fundraiser to build and sustain her endeavors; and so much more—seemingly all things to all people. But most of all, she was simply a mother. And today, we have gained a friend in Heaven, a woman of heroic virtue—a saint.

Don't let what you've read and reflected on in this book end your spiritual journey with Mother Cabrini. Carry her spirit and her voice with you. Come back to her words often and let them inspire you by her example of faith.

Mother Cabrini—St. Frances Xavier Cabrini—pray for us.

—*Crystalina Evert, founder, Women Made New!*

Source Material

Missionary Sisters of the Sacred Heart of Jesus. *Journal of a Trusting Heart: Retreat Notes of St. Frances Cabrini.* Chicago: Missionary Sisters of the Sacred Heart of Jesus, 1984.

———. *Travels of Mother Frances Xavier Cabrini.* Chicago: Missionary Sisters of the Sacred Heart of Jesus, 1944. https://archive.org/details/travelsofmotherfrancesxaviercabrini/mode/2up.

Introduction
"If the Sacred Heart would give me the means…"
Travels of Mother Frances Xavier Cabrini, Second Voyage to New York — April 1890, p. 3

"Your love must be active…"
Travels of Mother Frances Xavier Cabrini, Genoa to New York — September 1894, p. 60

"There was a time when Our Lord…"
Travels of Mother Frances Xavier Cabrini, Liverpool to New York — November 1898, p. 170

"'You are the light of the world…'"
Travels of Mother Frances Xavier Cabrini, Buenos Aires to Barcelona — August 1896, p. 145

"The days fly, souls are being lost."
Travels of Mother Frances Xavier Cabrini, Inauguration in Denver — November 1902, p. 237

"The Missionary knows no distance…"
Travels of Mother Frances Xavier Cabrini, New Orleans to Panama — May 1895, p. 105

"To-day the skin has begun to peel…"
Travels of Mother Frances Xavier Cabrini, Second Voyage to New York — April 1890, p. 11

"We seem to see the portals of Heaven…"
Travels of Mother Frances Xavier Cabrini, Genoa to New York — September 1894, p. 58

"Oh, sublime City…"
Travels of Mother Frances Xavier Cabrini, Genoa to New York — September 1894, p. 59

Week 1

"Let all your affections…"
Travels of Mother Frances Xavier Cabrini, Second Voyage to New York — April 1890, p. 3

"Oh, my daughters…"
Travels of Mother Frances Xavier Cabrini, Havre to New York — September 1891, p. 22

"Let us work…"
Travels of Mother Frances Xavier Cabrini, New York to Nicaragua — October 1891, p. 36

"We also made a little meditation…"
Travels of Mother Frances Xavier Cabrini, Second Voyage to New York — April 1890, p. 10

"Oh, happy the soul…"
Travels of Mother Frances Xavier Cabrini, Second Voyage to New York — April 1890, p. 10

Week 2

"This morning we went…"
Travels of Mother Frances Xavier Cabrini, Second Voyage to New York — April 1890, p. 3

"How many beautiful thoughts…"
Travels of Mother Frances Xavier Cabrini, Second Voyage to New York — April 1890, p. 4

"God commands, the sea obeys…"
Travels of Mother Frances Xavier Cabrini, Second Voyage to New York — April 1890, p. 5

"It seems as if Jesus Himself…"
Travels of Mother Frances Xavier Cabrini, Second Voyage to New York — April 1890, p. 5

Week 3

"At the sight of the sea…"
Travels of Mother Frances Xavier Cabrini, Second Voyage to New York — April 1890, p. 8

"Yes! Grace is an infinite treasure of God…"
Travels of Mother Frances Xavier Cabrini, Second Voyage to New York — April 1890, p. 8

"Let us try, oh, my daughters, to attract…"
Travels of Mother Frances Xavier Cabrini, Second Voyage to New York — April 1890, p. 8

"I write after having assisted…"
Travels of Mother Frances Xavier Cabrini, Second Voyage to New York — April 1890, p. 9

"The marvellous spectacle…"
Travels of Mother Frances Xavier Cabrini, Second Voyage to New York — April 1890, p. 9

"It is true the weather…"
Travels of Mother Frances Xavier Cabrini, New York to Havre — August 1890, p. 15

Week 4

"This morning I saw marvellous…"
Travels of Mother Frances Xavier Cabrini, New York to Havre — August 1890, p. 17

"Yesterday the sea…"
Travels of Mother Frances Xavier Cabrini, New York to Nicaragua — October 1891, p. 39

"To-day is the 15th…"
Travels of Mother Frances Xavier Cabrini, Genoa to New York — September 1894, p. 58

"The sea continues calm…"
Travels of Mother Frances Xavier Cabrini, New York to Havre — August 1890, p. 15

"Oh, sublime City, send down…"
Travels of Mother Frances Xavier Cabrini, Genoa to New York — September 1894, p. 59

"Just as we were passing…"
Travels of Mother Frances Xavier Cabrini, Genoa to New York — September 1894, p. 65

"Love the good God…"
Travels of Mother Frances Xavier Cabrini, Genoa to New York — September 1894, p. 71

Week 5

"We had Heaven in our hearts…"
Travels of Mother Frances Xavier Cabrini, Liverpool to New York — November 1898 p. 182

"Yesterday the fog was obstinate…"
Travels of Mother Frances Xavier Cabrini, London to New York — August 1902, p. 225

"They are the work…"
Travels of Mother Frances Xavier Cabrini, Letter to the Alumnae of Rome — May 1904, p. 247

Week 6

"To-day the skin has begun to peel…"
Travels of Mother Frances Xavier Cabrini, Second Voyage to New York — April 1890, p. 11

"Continue to be good…"
Travels of Mother Frances Xavier Cabrini, Second Voyage to New York — April 1890, p. 11

"The flames of human passions…"
Travels of Mother Frances Xavier Cabrini, Buenos Aires to Barcelona — August 1896, p. 155

"And you, dear daughters…"
Travels of Mother Frances Xavier Cabrini, New York to Havre — September 1899, p. 188

"Examine yourselves well…"
Travels of Mother Frances Xavier Cabrini, New York to Havre — September 1899, p. 188

Week 7

"A Protestant gentleman…"
Travels of Mother Frances Xavier Cabrini, Second Voyage to New York — April 1890, p. 11

"Yesterday we had a discussion…"
Travels of Mother Frances Xavier Cabrini, Second Voyage to New York — April 1890, p. 13

"Also another passenger…"
Travels of Mother Frances Xavier Cabrini, Second Voyage to New York — April 1890, p. 11

"Oh, let us pray, my daughters…"
Travels of Mother Frances Xavier Cabrini, Second Voyage to New York — April 1890, p. 12

Week 8

"I don't feel ill, but I am not well…"
Travels of Mother Frances Xavier Cabrini, New York to Havre — August 1890, p. 16

"Oh, if everyone had the knowledge…"
Travels of Mother Frances Xavier Cabrini, New York to Havre — August 1890, p. 16

"Let us love Jesus…"
Travels of Mother Frances Xavier Cabrini, New York to Havre — August 1890, p. 16

"On one occasion He said…"
Travels of Mother Frances Xavier Cabrini, New York to Havre — August 1890, p. 16

Week 9

"If the Sacred Heart would give me the means…"
Travels of Mother Frances Xavier Cabrini, Second Voyage to New York — April 1890, p3

"Zeal is a great charity…"
Journal of a Trusting Heart, p. 13

"When words have no effect…"
Journal of a Trusting Heart, p. 13

"Your love must be active…"
Travels of Mother Frances Xavier Cabrini, Genoa to New York — September 1894, p. 60

"Are you fearful?"
*Travels of Mother Frances
Xavier Cabrini*, Genoa to New
York — September 1894, p. 60

Week 10
"We are Missionaries, my
daughters…"
*Travels of Mother Frances Xavier
Cabrini*, New York to Havre — August
1890, p. 18

"For a Missionary, however difficult…"
*Travels of Mother Frances
Xavier Cabrini*, Havre to New
York — September 1891, p. 33

"Then once more we rowed…"
*Travels of Mother Frances
Xavier Cabrini*, New York to
Nicaragua — October 1891, p. 47

"I would like to convert all
Protestants."
*Travels of Mother Frances Xavier
Cabrini*, New York to Havre — August
1890, p. 17

"The Protestant lady never leaves us."
*Travels of Mother Frances Xavier
Cabrini*, New York to Havre — August
1890, p. 17

Week 11
"Oh, blessed voice…"
*Travels of Mother Frances
Xavier Cabrini*, New York to
Nicaragua — October 1891, p. 48

"Even here on board ladies.."
*Travels of Mother Frances
Xavier Cabrini*, New York to
Nicaragua — October 1891, p. 49

"Our great Patron, Saint Francis
Xavier…"
*Travels of Mother Frances
Xavier Cabrini*, New York to
Nicaragua — October 1891, p. 53

Week 12
"We left Gibraltar…"
*Travels of Mother Frances
Xavier Cabrini*, Genoa to New
York — September 1894, p. 60

"The harvest is great…"
*Travels of Mother Frances
Xavier Cabrini*, Genoa to New
York — September 1894, p. 60

"Oh, dear Jesus, what terrible ruin!"
*Travels of Mother Frances
Xavier Cabrini*, Buenos Aires to
Barcelona — August 1896, p. 155

"O Jesus, the Desired of Ages…"
*Travels of Mother Frances
Xavier Cabrini*, Buenos Aires to
Barcelona — August 1896, p. 155

"Thou art my life…"
*Travels of Mother Frances
Xavier Cabrini*, Buenos Aires to
Barcelona — August 1896, p. 155

Week 13

"There was a time…"
Travels of Mother Frances Xavier Cabrini, Liverpool to New York — November 1898, p. 169

"Pray, dear daughters…"
Travels of Mother Frances Xavier Cabrini, Liverpool to New York — November 1898, pp. 170–171

"Let us open wide our hearts…"
Travels of Mother Frances Xavier Cabrini, New York to Havre — September 1899, p. 187

Week 14

"Let us imagine…"
Travels of Mother Frances Xavier Cabrini, Genoa to Buenos Aires — December 1900, p. 198

"The days fly…"
Travels of Mother Frances Xavier Cabrini, Inauguration in Denver — November 1902, p. 237

"Work, then, while…"
Travels of Mother Frances Xavier Cabrini, Inauguration in Denver — November 1902, p. 237

"Seek amongst your acquaintances…"
Travels of Mother Frances Xavier Cabrini, Inauguration in Denver — November 1902, p. 237

"How many beautiful souls…"
Travels of Mother Frances Xavier Cabrini, Inauguration in Denver — November 1902, p. 237

"The first condition is prayer."
Travels of Mother Frances Xavier Cabrini, Inauguration in Denver — November 1902, p. 237

"What is given to the Missionary…"
Travels of Mother Frances Xavier Cabrini, Inauguration in Denver — November 1902, pp. 237–238

Week 15

"The Colonel came on deck…"
Travels of Mother Frances Xavier Cabrini, New York to Nicaragua — October 1891, p. 44

"Let the Blessed Virgin…"
Travels of Mother Frances Xavier Cabrini, New York to Nicaragua — October 1891, pp. 45–46

"Poor souls!"
Travels of Mother Frances Xavier Cabrini, Letter to the Alumnae of Rome — May 1904, p. 244

"Let us be generous…"
Travels of Mother Frances Xavier Cabrini, Letter to the Alumnae of Rome — May 1904, pp. 244–245

Source Material

Week 16
"Worldlings look with esteem…"
*Travels of Mother Frances
Xavier Cabrini*, Genoa to New
York — September 1894, p. 61

"Virgins are chosen…"
*Travels of Mother Frances
Xavier Cabrini*, Genoa to New
York — September 1894, p. 61

"Come, prudent Virgins…"
*Travels of Mother Frances
Xavier Cabrini*, Genoa to New
York — September 1894, p. 61

"He who calls us…"
*Travels of Mother Frances
Xavier Cabrini*, Genoa to New
York — September 1894, p. 61

"To this beautiful soul consecrated…"
*Travels of Mother Frances
Xavier Cabrini*, Genoa to New
York — September 1894, p. 63

Week 17
"You, the chosen portions…"
*Travels of Mother Frances
Xavier Cabrini*, New Orleans to
Panama — May 1895, p. 77

"The conversion of sinners…"
*Travels of Mother Frances
Xavier Cabrini*, New Orleans to
Panama — May 1895, p. 85

"How pleasing it is…"
*Travels of Mother Frances
Xavier Cabrini*, New Orleans to
Panama — May 1895, p. 96

"May the Holy Spirit…"
*Travels of Mother Frances
Xavier Cabrini*, New Orleans to
Panama — May 1895, p. 96

Week 18
"And you, my dear daughters…"
*Travels of Mother Frances
Xavier Cabrini*, New Orleans to
Panama — May 1895, p. 105

"'You are the light of the world…'"
*Travels of Mother Frances
Xavier Cabrini*, Buenos Aires to
Barcelona — August 1896, p. 145

"Reflecting upon my vocation…"
*Travels of Mother Frances
Xavier Cabrini*, New York to
Havre — September 1899, pp.
185–186

"Vast and fruitful…"
*Travels of Mother Frances
Xavier Cabrini*, New York to
Havre — September 1899, p. 186

"Do continual violence…"
*Travels of Mother Frances
Xavier Cabrini*, New York to
Havre — September 1899, p. 186

Week 19

"Remember, daughters, you are the tutelary…"
Travels of Mother Frances Xavier Cabrini, New York to Havre — September 1899, p. 188

"Always renew your offering…"
Travels of Mother Frances Xavier Cabrini, New York to Havre — September 1899, p. 189

"She who consecrates herself…"
Travels of Mother Frances Xavier Cabrini, Letter to the Students — February 1906, pp. 266–267

Week 20

"For, unfortunately, [the passengers]…"
Travels of Mother Frances Xavier Cabrini, Second Voyage to New York — April 1890, p. 12

"Sister Bernardina is going…"
Travels of Mother Frances Xavier Cabrini, Second Voyage to New York — April 1890, p. 14

"A Freemason, who, as soon…"
Travels of Mother Frances Xavier Cabrini, New Orleans to Panama — May 1895, p. 90

"Here, however, we…"
Travels of Mother Frances Xavier Cabrini, New Orleans to Panama — May 1895, p. 90

Week 21

"The devil has placed…"
Travels of Mother Frances Xavier Cabrini, New Orleans to Panama — May 1895, p. 91

"See how dangerous these times…"
Travels of Mother Frances Xavier Cabrini, Panama to Buenos Aires — October 1895, p. 128

"We have occasion to feel great…"
Travels of Mother Frances Xavier Cabrini, Genoa to Buenos Aires — December 1900, p. 206

"Oh, daughters, let us render…"
Travels of Mother Frances Xavier Cabrini, Genoa to Buenos Aires — December 1900, p. 206

Week 22

"The world is poisoned…"
Travels of Mother Frances Xavier Cabrini, Inauguration in Denver — November 1902, p. 236

"Our good God…"
Travels of Mother Frances Xavier Cabrini, Letter to the Alumnae of Rome — May 1905, p. 252

"Oh, if the voice of religion…"
Travels of Mother Frances Xavier Cabrini, Letter to the Students — February 1906, p. 263

"Pray, my good daughters…"
Travels of Mother Frances Xavier Cabrini, Letter to the Students — February 1906, p. 264

Week 23

"Pray that all the docile…"
Travels of Mother Frances Xavier Cabrini, Letter to the Students — February 1906, p. 264

"Take religion away…"
Travels of Mother Frances Xavier Cabrini, Letter to the Students — February 1906, p. 276

"In union with Your painful…"
Journal of a Trusting Heart, p. 12

Week 24

"Yesterday, the 21st…"
Travels of Mother Frances Xavier Cabrini, New York to Nicaragua — October 1891, p. 48

"It is only one day…"
Travels of Mother Frances Xavier Cabrini, Genoa to New York — September 1894, p. 58

"We are in the bosom…"
Travels of Mother Frances Xavier Cabrini, Genoa to New York — September 1894, p. 58

"So, here again…"
Travels of Mother Frances Xavier Cabrini, Genoa to New York — September 1894, p. 60

"The heavens were so clouded…"
Travels of Mother Frances Xavier Cabrini, Panama to Buenos Aires — October 1895, p. 111

Week 25

"I never felt the bitterness…"
Travels of Mother Frances Xavier Cabrini, Havre to New York — September 1891, p. 21

"Fresh water and salty water…"
Travels of Mother Frances Xavier Cabrini, Genoa to New York — September 1894, p. 72

Week 26

"As long as we remain…"
Travels of Mother Frances Xavier Cabrini, Liverpool to New York — November 1898, p. 163

"We may have to suffer…"
Travels of Mother Frances Xavier Cabrini, Liverpool to New York — November 1898, p. 163

"Learn how to unite…"
Travels of Mother Frances Xavier Cabrini, Liverpool to New York — November 1898, p. 163

"In suffering for Jesus…"
Travels of Mother Frances Xavier Cabrini, Liverpool to New York — November 1898, pp. 163–164

"Yes, yes, loveable Jesus…"
Journal of a Trusting Heart, p. 11

"Lord, unite me intimately…"
Journal of a Trusting Heart, p. 11

Week 27

"I will not distinguish between…"
Journal of a Trusting Heart, p. 21

"Persecutions will never…"
Journal of a Trusting Heart, pp. 21–22

"Outwardly I will not show…"
Journal of a Trusting Heart, p. 30

"All for Jesus, all with Jesus…"
Journal of a Trusting Heart, p. 30

"I am created by God…"
Journal of a Trusting Heart, p. 58

"I will try never to complain…"
Journal of a Trusting Heart, pp. 58–59

"In the heart where…"
Journal of a Trusting Heart, p. 59

"The sacrament of Penance…"
Journal of a Trusting Heart, p. 13

"The sacrament of Penance…"
Journal of a Trusting Heart, p. 13

Week 28

"Mary is most holy…"
Travels of Mother Frances Xavier Cabrini, Havre to New York — September 1891, p. 25

"What an admirable model…"
Travels of Mother Frances Xavier Cabrini, Havre to New York — September 1891, p. 25

"My God, may all souls…"
Travels of Mother Frances Xavier Cabrini, Havre to New York — September 1891, p. 25

"Mary knew her mission…"
Travels of Mother Frances Xavier Cabrini, Havre to New York — September 1891, p. 25

"Let us strive, O daughters…"
Travels of Mother Frances Xavier Cabrini, Havre to New York — September 1891, p. 25

"All the glory of the King's…"
Travels of Mother Frances Xavier Cabrini, Havre to New York — September 1891, p. 26

"Have faith, lively faith…"
Travels of Mother Frances Xavier Cabrini, Havre to New York — September 1891, p. 26

Week 29

"Oh, how good is Mary!"
Travels of Mother Frances Xavier Cabrini, New York to Nicaragua — October 1891, p. 38

"This morning the rainbow…"
Travels of Mother Frances Xavier Cabrini, Genoa to New York — September 1894, p. 66

"Mary, our sweet Mother…"
Travels of Mother Frances Xavier Cabrini, Genoa to New York — September 1894, p. 66

"Mary is like the beautiful…"
Travels of Mother Frances
Xavier Cabrini, Genoa to New
York — September 1894, p. 66

"As a cloud brightened…"
Travels of Mother Frances
Xavier Cabrini, Genoa to New
York — September 1894, p. 72

"Sweet mother, you…"
Journal of a Trusting Heart, p. 56

"I will study all ways…"
Journal of a Trusting Heart, p. 61

Week 30
"Mary is the Mysterious Book…"
Travels of Mother Frances
Xavier Cabrini, Genoa to New
York — September 1894, p. 73

"Mary speaks to you plainly…"
Travels of Mother Frances
Xavier Cabrini, Genoa to New
York — September 1894, p. 73

"She is dressed in blue and white…"
Travels of Mother Frances
Xavier Cabrini, Buenos Aires to
Barcelona — August 1896,
pp. 145–146

"And the help. needed…"
Travels of Mother Frances
Xavier Cabrini, Buenos Aires to
Barcelona — August 1896, p. 146

"Oh, the greatness of Mary!"
Travels of Mother Frances
Xavier Cabrini, Buenos Aires to
Barcelona — August 1896, p. 153

Week 31
"The Areopagite spoke…"
Travels of Mother Frances
Xavier Cabrini, Buenos Aires to
Barcelona — August 1896, p. 146

"How beautiful it is…"
Travels of Mother Frances
Xavier Cabrini, Buenos Aires to
Barcelona — August 1896, p. 148

"Mary, O children…"
Travels of Mother Frances
Xavier Cabrini, Buenos Aires to
Barcelona — August 1896,
pp. 153–154

"If you desire to convert…"
Travels of Mother Frances
Xavier Cabrini, Buenos Aires to
Barcelona — August 1896, p. 154

"Yes, you can do everything…"
Travels of Mother Frances
Xavier Cabrini, Buenos Aires to
Barcelona — August 1896, p. 154

"In order to be faithful…"
Travels of Mother Frances
Xavier Cabrini, New York to
Havre — September 1899, p. 193

"Oh! dear Mother…"
Travels of Mother Frances
Xavier Cabrini, New York to
Havre — September 1899, p. 193

"Shower upon us thy blessings…"
Travels of Mother Frances
Xavier Cabrini, New York to
Havre — September 1899, p. 193

Week 32

"How beautiful is Mary!"
Travels of Mother Frances
Xavier Cabrini, Genoa to Buenos
Aires — December 1900, p. 203

"Oh, how good…"
Travels of Mother Frances
Xavier Cabrini, Buenos Aires to
Barcelona — August 1896, p. 153

"What shall we fear, daughters…"
Travels of Mother Frances
Xavier Cabrini, Genoa to Buenos
Aires — December 1900, p. 203

"She is, indeed…"
Travels of Mother Frances
Xavier Cabrini, Genoa to Buenos
Aires — December 1900, p. 203

"Mary lived more…"
Travels of Mother Frances
Xavier Cabrini, Genoa to Buenos
Aires — December 1900, pp. 203–204

"And to-day, oh, daughters…"
Travels of Mother Frances
Xavier Cabrini, Genoa to Buenos
Aires — December 1900, p. 204

"But I should never finish…"
Travels of Mother Frances
Xavier Cabrini, Genoa to Buenos
Aires — December 1900, p. 204

"When your weaknesses…"
Travels of Mother Frances
Xavier Cabrini, Genoa to Buenos
Aires — December 1900, p. 204

Week 33

"See how grateful…"
*Travels of Mother Frances Xavier
Cabrini*, Letter to the Alumnae of
Rome — May 1904, p. 245

"But Mary appeared…"
*Travels of Mother Frances Xavier
Cabrini*, Letter to the Alumnae of
Rome — May 1904, p. 245

"All this we owe…"
*Travels of Mother Frances Xavier
Cabrini*, Letter to the Alumnae of
Rome — May 1904, p. 245

"Mary derives all…"
*Travels of Mother Frances Xavier
Cabrini*, Letter to the Alumnae of
Rome — May 1904, p. 245

"If, then, we wish…"
Travels of Mother Frances Xavier Cabrini,
Letter to the Alumnae of Rome — May 1904, pp. 245–246

"Cast an interior glance…"
Travels of Mother Frances Xavier Cabrini, Letter to the Alumnae of Rome — May 1904, p. 246

Week 34

"Holy Church in her…"
Travels of Mother Frances Xavier Cabrini, Letter to the Alumnae of Rome — May 1904, p. 246

"Saint Ambrose says…"
Travels of Mother Frances Xavier Cabrini, Letter to the Alumnae of Rome — May 1904, p. 246

"The difficulties of the primitive…"
Travels of Mother Frances Xavier Cabrini, Letter to the Alumnae of Rome — May 1904, p. 246

"Let us call upon Mary…"
Travels of Mother Frances Xavier Cabrini, Letter to the Alumnae of Rome — May 1904, pp. 246–247

"How admirable is Mary…"
Travels of Mother Frances Xavier Cabrini, Letter to the Alumnae of Rome — May 1904, p. 247

"Dressed in rose gown…"
Journal of a Trusting Heart, p. 1

Week 35

"Behold that Divine Heart!"
Travels of Mother Frances Xavier Cabrini, New York to Havre — August 1890, p. 19

"Let us seek the right…"
Travels of Mother Frances Xavier Cabrini, New York to Nicaragua — October 1891, p. 41

"Blessed Margaret Mary Alacoque…"
Travels of Mother Frances Xavier Cabrini, New York to Nicaragua — October 1891, pp. 41–42

"Little time remains…"
Travels of Mother Frances Xavier Cabrini, New York to Nicaragua — October 1891, p. 42

Week 36

"Love ought to transform…"
Travels of Mother Frances Xavier Cabrini, New Orleans to Panama — May 1895, p. 92

"The good Jesus…"
Travels of Mother Frances Xavier Cabrini, New Orleans to Panama — May 1895, pp. 92–93

"Let us throw ourselves…"
Travels of Mother Frances Xavier Cabrini, New Orleans to Panama — May 1895, p. 93

"And what may we not…"
Travels of Mother Frances Xavier Cabrini, New Orleans to Panama — May 1895, p. 93

"Very often our prayers…"
Travels of Mother Frances Xavier Cabrini, New Orleans to Panama — May 1895, p. 93

"Through your goodness…"
Journal of a Trusting Heart, p. 75

Week 37

"In the secrecy of the Holy…"
Travels of Mother Frances Xavier Cabrini, New Orleans to Panama — May 1895, p. 93

"Recall often what…"
Travels of Mother Frances Xavier Cabrini, New Orleans to Panama — May 1895, pp. 93–94

"Let us fly, fly…"
Travels of Mother Frances Xavier Cabrini, New Orleans to Panama — May 1895, p. 94

Week 38

"By the words of consecration…"
Travels of Mother Frances Xavier Cabrini, New Orleans to Panama — May 1895, p. 94

"As long as the species…"
Travels of Mother Frances Xavier Cabrini, New Orleans to Panama — May 1895, p. 94

"Our Savior hides…"
Journal of a Trusting Heart, p. 105

"Let us pray to…"
Journal of a Trusting Heart, p. 105

"Frequent spiritual communions…"
Journal of a Trusting Heart, p. 105

"In the Holy Eucharist…"
Journal of a Trusting Heart, p. 107

Week 39

"Last night the weather…"
Travels of Mother Frances Xavier Cabrini, Havre to New York — September 1891, p. 28

"Let us learn, dear daughters…"
Travels of Mother Frances Xavier Cabrini, Havre to New York — September 1891, p. 28

"No, daughters, God…"
Travels of Mother Frances Xavier Cabrini, Havre to New York — September 1891, p. 28

"Oh, humility, how powerful…"
Travels of Mother Frances Xavier Cabrini, New York to Nicaragua — October 1891, p. 43

"Be grateful of God's mercies…"
Travels of Mother Frances Xavier Cabrini, New York to Nicaragua — October 1891, pp. 42–43

"With humility, you will…"
Travels of Mother Frances Xavier Cabrini, New York to Nicaragua — October 1891, p. 43

"Humility is the foundation…"
Journal of a Trusting Heart, p. 112

Week 40

"Humility is the secret…"
Travels of Mother Frances Xavier Cabrini, Genoa to New York — September 1894, p. 69

"The humblest obtain…"
Travels of Mother Frances Xavier Cabrini, Genoa to New York — September 1894, p. 69

"It is in Retreat…"
Travels of Mother Frances Xavier Cabrini, Liverpool to New York — November 1898, pp. 166–167

"Let us weigh carefully…"
Travels of Mother Frances Xavier Cabrini, Liverpool to New York — November 1898, p. 167

"Be, therefore, watchful…"
Travels of Mother Frances Xavier Cabrini, Liverpool to New York — November 1898, p. 167

"Many often complain…"
Travels of Mother Frances Xavier Cabrini, Liverpool to New York — November 1898, p. 167

Week 41

"Oh, obedience…"
Travels of Mother Frances Xavier Cabrini, Havre to New York — September 1891, p. 27

"Oh, happy obedience!"
Travels of Mother Frances Xavier Cabrini, Havre to New York — September 1891, p. 27

"None of you should…"
Travels of Mother Frances Xavier Cabrini, Havre to New York — September 1891, p. 27

"Do not have any will…"
Travels of Mother Frances Xavier Cabrini, Havre to New York — September 1891, pp. 27–28

"In martyrdom…"
Travels of Mother Frances Xavier Cabrini, Genoa to New York — September 1894, p. 63

"Saint Mary Magdalen…"
Travels of Mother Frances Xavier Cabrini, Genoa to New York — September 1894, p. 63

"To share the love…"
Journal of a Trusting Heart, p. f

Week 42

"Every time we come…"
Travels of Mother Frances Xavier Cabrini, Havre to New York — September 1891, p. 29

"Oh, would that God…"
Travels of Mother Frances Xavier Cabrini, Havre to New York — September 1891, p. 30

"Our faith obliges…"
Travels of Mother Frances Xavier Cabrini, Genoa to New York — September 1894, p. 67

"Be faithful to what…"
Travels of Mother Frances Xavier Cabrini, New Orleans to Panama — May 1895, p. 81

"The Holy Prophet David…"
Travels of Mother Frances Xavier Cabrini, New Orleans to Panama — May 1895, p. 81

"Blessed will you be…"
Travels of Mother Frances Xavier Cabrini, New Orleans to Panama — May 1895, p. 81

Week 43
"Remember, daughters, that…"
Travels of Mother Frances Xavier Cabrini, Liverpool to New York — November 1898, p. 175

"We are dedicated…"
Travels of Mother Frances Xavier Cabrini, Liverpool to New York — November 1898, p. 175

"Ask Him to seal…"
Travels of Mother Frances Xavier Cabrini, Liverpool to New York — November 1898, p. 175

"Let us have confidence…"
Travels of Mother Frances Xavier Cabrini, Liverpool to New York — November 1898, p. 177

"Thanksgiving is a perfect…"
Travels of Mother Frances Xavier Cabrini, New York to Havre — September 1899, pp. 190–191

"The flame of the love…"
Travels of Mother Frances Xavier Cabrini, New York to Havre — September 1899, p. 192

"Be faithful. Leave…"
Travels of Mother Frances Xavier Cabrini, New York to Havre — September 1899, p. 192

Week 44
"We, leaning on our Beloved…"
Travels of Mother Frances Xavier Cabrini, New York to Havre — September 1899, p. 194

"Oh, yes, the Missionary…"
Travels of Mother Frances Xavier Cabrini, London to New York — August 1902, p. 220

"Always appreciate the…"
*Travels of Mother Frances
Xavier Cabrini*, London to New
York — August 1902, p. 220

"At the end of the Retreat…"
*Travels of Mother Frances
Xavier Cabrini*, London to New
York — August 1902, pp. 220–221

Week 45
"Remember, however, dear…"
*Travels of Mother Frances
Xavier Cabrini*, London to New
York — August 1902, p. 223

"My heart is ready, O God…"
Journal of a Trusting Heart, p. 16

"To lose confidence in God…"
Journal of a Trusting Heart, p. 21

"It is really sad…"
*Travels of Mother Frances
Xavier Cabrini*, Havre to New
York — September 1891, p. 31

"Yes, if there is true…"
*Travels of Mother Frances
Xavier Cabrini*, Havre to New
York — September 1891, pp. 31–32

Week 46
"'But I am weak…'"
*Travels of Mother Frances Xavier
Cabrini*, Panama to Buenos
Aires — October 1895, p. 109

"In order not to fall…"
Journal of a Trusting Heart, p. 17

"The faults of which…"
Journal of a Trusting Heart, p. 17

"Without the practice…"
Journal of a Trusting Heart, p. 18

"Let us also be faithful…"
*Travels of Mother Frances
Xavier Cabrini*, New York to
Nicaragua — October 1891, p. 41

Week 47
"How fruitful is…"
*Travels of Mother Frances
Xavier Cabrini*, New Orleans to
Panama — May 1895, pp. 83–84

"The Pope is the shining lighthouse…"
*Travels of Mother Frances Xavier
Cabrini*, Liverpool to New
York — November 1898, p. 162

"These Blessed Souls cannot…"
*Travels of Mother Frances
Xavier Cabrini*, Genoa to New
York — September 1894, pp. 69–70

"Have no fear that…"
*Travels of Mother Frances
Xavier Cabrini*, Genoa to New
York — September 1894, p. 70

"Be generous to…"
*Travels of Mother Frances
Xavier Cabrini*, Genoa to New
York — September 1894, p. 70

Week 48

"What a gift…"
Travels of Mother Frances Xavier Cabrini, Panama to Buenos Aires — October 1895, p. 115

"Prayer is powerful!"
Travels of Mother Frances Xavier Cabrini, Buenos Aires to Barcelona — August 1896, p. 158

"Love us, Jesus…"
Travels of Mother Frances Xavier Cabrini, Liverpool to New York — November 1898, p. 161

"'I will lead my beloved…'"
Travels of Mother Frances Xavier Cabrini, Liverpool to New York — November 1898, pp. 165–166

"God is a most pure…"
Travels of Mother Frances Xavier Cabrini, Liverpool to New York — November 1898, p. 166

"It is in Retreat…"
Travels of Mother Frances Xavier Cabrini, Liverpool to New York — November 1898, p. 166

"Now, here is the second…"
Travels of Mother Frances Xavier Cabrini, Letter to the Alumnae of Rome — May 1905, p. 252

Week 49

"Those souls united in…"
Travels of Mother Frances Xavier Cabrini, Genoa to New York — September 1894, p. 71

"What a wonderful sight…"
Travels of Mother Frances Xavier Cabrini, Genoa to New York — September 1894, pp. 71–72

"Though Charity signifies…"
Travels of Mother Frances Xavier Cabrini, New Orleans to Panama — May 1895, p. 79

"So, to pray we must…"
Travels of Mother Frances Xavier Cabrini, New Orleans to Panama — May 1895, p. 79

"Oh, if I could but…"
Travels of Mother Frances Xavier Cabrini, New Orleans to Panama — May 1895, p. 88

"Whenever, due to my…"
Journal of a Trusting Heart, p. 34

"Jesus, envelop me in…"
Journal of a Trusting Heart, p. 78

Week 50

"May God bless you…"
Travels of Mother Frances Xavier Cabrini, Panama to Buenos Aires — October 1895, pp. 142–143

"Do not seek rest…"
*Travels of Mother Frances Xavier
Cabrini*, Panama to Buenos
Aires — October 1895, p. 143

"Now that the voyage…"
*Travels of Mother Frances
Xavier Cabrini*, Genoa to New
York — September 1894, p. 74

"The Holy Prophet…"
*Travels of Mother Frances
Xavier Cabrini*, Genoa to New
York — September 1894, pp. 74–75

Week 51

"My beloved is more…"
Journal of a Trusting Heart, pp. 47–48

"The soul perfectly abandoned…"
Journal of a Trusting Heart, p. 71

"We seem to see…"
*Travels of Mother Frances
Xavier Cabrini*, Genoa to New
York — September 1894, pp. 58–59

Week 52

"I wanted to go…"
*Travels of Mother Frances
Xavier Cabrini*, Genoa to New
York — September 1894, p. 75

"I found everything…"
*Travels of Mother Frances
Xavier Cabrini*, Genoa to New
York — September 1894, p. 75

"In the meantime…"
*Travels of Mother Frances
Xavier Cabrini*, Genoa to New
York — September 1894, p. 75

Biography of
Mother Cabrini

By Michael Lichens

Maria Francesca Cabrini was born in Lombardy, Italy, on July 15, 1850, the youngest of thirteen children. Raised in a devout home, the young Francesca dreamed of growing up to be a missionary to China and other lands. She would launch paper boats filled with violets that she pretended were missionaries on their way to far-off lands. At thirteen, she began studying with the Daughters of the Sacred Heart of Jesus and graduated with high honors.

After graduation, Francesca helped with her family and obtained a teaching certificate. After her mother's death in 1870, she desired to become a nun and applied for admission to the Daughters of the Sacred Heart, her old teachers. Unfortunately, the nuns rejected Francesca on account of her ill health. Still, she felt God's calling and wanted to find a way to become a nun and missionary.

Francesca taught school for several years, where she met her spiritual mentor and friend, Msgr. Antonio Serrati. Learning about her ambitions, Msgr. Serrati asked the young Francesca to work with the children at the House of Providence orphanage. At the age of twenty-four, Francesca began teaching at the House of Providence, which was suffering under poor leadership.

In 1877, Francesca took religious vows and started attracting other nuns. In honor of the Jesuit missionary St. Francis Xavier, she took the name Frances Xavier (Francesca Saverio), showing that her missionary ambitions had never waned. In 1880, she and seven other nuns founded their order, the Missionary Sisters of the Sacred Heart of Jesus (MSC). Mother Cabrini's mission was initially restricted to Northern Italy, where she established several schools and orphanages.

Mother Cabrini's good works got the attention of bishops and even of Pope Leo XIII. Still, she desired to be a missionary to China and was persistent in preparation for such a mission. However, she was now being called to the United States. At the encouragement of Msgr. Serrati and the pope, she and a few other nuns set off for New York, arriving on March 31, 1889. Here, she truly began her international missionary work.

Her work was met with great difficulties from the beginning. Mother Cabrini did not receive a warm welcome from the archbishop and the other city officials. At the time, Italian immigrants were regarded with suspicion and animosity. Undeterred, Mother Cabrini sought to help her fellow immigrants in Little Italy and other communities.

Mother Cabrini taught catechism classes and saw to the needs of the orphaned children. She soon obtained permission to open her first orphanage in the Americas in West Park, New York. Throughout this experience, she acted as an administrator and fundraiser for her order, often walking the streets to ask for donations. These works and her resourcefulness won over many people in her lifetime.

In 1896, Mother Cabrini opened Columbus Hospital in New York, the first of many hospitals that she established. Thanks to her administrative acumen, Mother Cabrini and the Missionary

Sisters established religious, educational, and health institutions throughout the United States, South America, and Europe. She personally established many of these institutions, traveling by steamship dozens of times and even taking a mule across the Andes mountains. Many of these institutions still function today.

Mother Cabrini became a U.S. citizen in 1909, but her missionary work continued to have a global impact. While her work was originally among Italian immigrants, her order attracted vocations from around the world. With thousands of nuns in her order, she was constantly expanding her work.

At the age of sixty-seven, Mother Cabrini died on December 22, 1917. She died in the hospital she founded in Chicago. Due to her holiness and great work, her cause of beatification was opened soon after her death. Meanwhile, the global work of her Missionary Sisters of the Sacred Heart continues.

Mother Cabrini was beatified in 1938 and was canonized in 1946 by Pope Pius XII, becoming the first American citizen to be declared a saint. St. Frances Xavier Cabrini's feast day is November 13, and she is the patron saint of immigrants. Her major shrines can be found in New York, Chicago, and Colorado, but there are minor shrines and memorials to her in the dozens of cities she worked in and visited.

About the Author

Kristen Van Uden Theriault earned a B.A. in history and Russian area studies at Saint Anselm College. She trained in oral history and began researching the experience of Catholics who survived, escaped, or resisted communist regimes.

She then worked as an apprentice in oral history at the Earl Gregg Swem Library's Special Collections Research Center at the College of William & Mary, where she completed her M.A. in history.

She researches Catholics who survived totalitarianism in the twentieth century. She is especially interested in pursuing this subject through the historiographies of Catholic martyrdom, memory studies, and dissident literature.

She currently works at Sophia Institute Press as a media spokesperson and has been featured on a wide variety of media platforms such as *First Things*, Sensus Fidelium, and Coast to Coast AM. She is also the editor of Catholic Exchange.

Sophia Institute

Sophia Institute is a nonprofit institution that seeks to nurture the spiritual, moral, and cultural life of souls and to spread the gospel of Christ in conformity with the authentic teachings of the Roman Catholic Church.

Sophia Institute Press fulfills this mission by offering translations, reprints, and new publications that afford readers a rich source of the enduring wisdom of mankind.

Sophia Institute also operates the popular online resource CatholicExchange.com. *Catholic Exchange* provides world news from a Catholic perspective as well as daily devotionals and articles that will help readers to grow in holiness and live a life consistent with the teachings of the Church.

In 2013, Sophia Institute launched Sophia Institute for Teachers to renew and rebuild Catholic culture through service to Catholic education. With the goal of nurturing the spiritual, moral, and cultural life of souls, and an abiding respect for the role and work of teachers, we strive to provide materials and programs that are at once enlightening to the mind and ennobling to the heart; faithful and complete, as well as useful and practical.

Sophia Institute gratefully recognizes the Solidarity Association for preserving and encouraging the growth of our apostolate over the course of many years. Without their generous and timely support, this book would not be in your hands.

www.SophiaInstitute.com
www.CatholicExchange.com
www.SophiaInstituteforTeachers.org

Sophia Institute Press is a registered trademark of Sophia Institute.
Sophia Institute is a tax-exempt institution as defined by the
Internal Revenue Code, Section 501(c)(3). Tax ID 22-2548708.